CLEVER ONE POT

Fabulous fuss-free food

DAIRY COOKBOOK

CONTENTS

Introduction

In the twenty-first century life flies past at a tremendous pace.
We all have too much to do and not enough time to do it.

However, this doesn't mean that we all need to eat ready meals. And if you are reading this, it means that you don't want to live on convenience food, but you are someone who wants to cook real, nutritious and delicious food.

With Clever One Pot everyone can create tasty meals in a short space of time with little washing up (or pans cluttering your dishwasher). One pot meals are the original convenience food and feature in virtually every cuisine around the world.

Why Clever?

So why is this book 'clever'? Well, naturally, this book provides a wealth of recipes that require only one cooking pot, but they also create a COMPLETE meal. Some recipes don't need any side dishes, but if required, each recipe will suggest an accompaniment that does not need an extra cooking pot (something that many 'one pot' books omit). As with all Dairy Cookbooks, all the ingredients should be readily available in your local supermarket. Or if you choose to shop on the high street, you should find everything you need in the butchers, greengrocer and delicatessen.

Every single recipe has been triple-tested; by food professionals and by normal cooks in their homes, to ensure that each and every one is perfect first time!
To make life easier, we have split the chapters into two – Quick & Easy and Take it Easy. They feature recipes that are straightforward and none of the them takes hours of preparation but the Quick & Easy recipes can be on the table within half an hour – ideal for after work cooking, whilst the Take it Easy recipes require longer cooking – providing scrumptious stews and bakes that are cooked to perfection.

Put simply, this book helps you to
create fabulous food without fuss.

Recipe Notes

Serves: Each recipe will suggest how many it will serve, though of course this does depend on size of portion preferred.

Nutritional information: Every recipe also shows nutritional information, calculated per portion by a fully qualified nutritional consultant. Where the recipe gives a range of servings e.g. 4-6, the calories, fat and saturated fat will have been calculated on the higher number of servings.

Time: It will also give the amount of time taken to finish the dish, including any preparation time.

The **V** symbol shows that the recipe is suitable for vegetarians, provided that you use an appropriate type of cheese or yogurt. A few dairy products use animal rennet or gelatine, so it's best to check the label.

The **F** symbol shows that the recipe is suitable for freezing. So if you are cooking for fewer people than the recipe suggests you can freeze what is left over. Allow the dish to cool, then fill a container and pop in the freezer –et voilà two meals with very little effort! Ensure you allow it to defrost fully before heating gently until piping hot.

Why QR Codes?

What do you fancy for dinner tonight?

Simply choose a recipe, scan the QR code with your smartphone and it will provide you with a list of ingredients.

Pop to the shops and you have a list to hand while you are shopping – simple!

The list is embedded in the QR code, which means it is stored on your phone – no internet connection required.

If you haven't already done so, you will need to download a QR scanner app for your phone. These are usually free and readily available from your favourite app store.

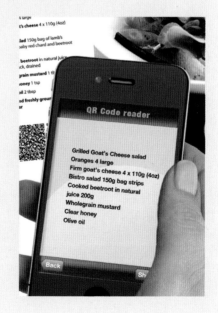

SOUPS

Tomato Soup Ⓥ Ⓕ

Time 30 mins. Per portion: 286 Kcal
19g fat (10.9g saturated). Serves 2

butter 25g (1oz)
onion 1, peeled and chopped
carrot 1, peeled and chopped
chopped tomatoes 400g can
tomato purée 1 tbsp
vegetable stock 300ml (½ pint)
caster sugar 1 tsp

Melt the butter in a saucepan over a medium heat. Add the onion and carrot and cook for 5–7 minutes until softened.

Add the chopped tomatoes, tomato purée, stock and caster sugar to the pan, cover with a lid and bring to the boil. Then reduce the heat and simmer for 10–15 minutes until the vegetables are really tender.

Remove from the heat and purée the soup using a hand-held stick blender.

Tomato & Pepper Soup Ⓥ Ⓕ

Time 20 mins. Per portion: 159 Kcal
11g fat (1.2g saturated). Serves 4

olive oil 3 tbsp
red peppers 2, deseeded and chopped
red onion 1 small, peeled and chopped
garlic 1 clove, peeled and chopped
chopped tomatoes 400g can
sun-dried tomato paste 2 tbsp
vegetable stock 750ml (1¼ pints)
basil 25g (1oz)
freshly ground black pepper

Heat the oil in a large saucepan over a medium heat. Add the peppers and onion and cook for 5 minutes until softened. Add the garlic, tomatoes, tomato paste and stock and bring to the boil. Reduce the heat and cook gently for 2 minutes.

Remove the pan from the heat, add the basil and purée the soup using a hand-held stick blender. Season to taste and serve.

Creamy Cauliflower Soup Ⓥ Ⓕ

Time 20 mins. Per portion: 165 Kcal
8g fat (3.8g saturated). Serves 4

butter 15g (½oz)
cauliflower ½, broken into florets
onion 1 small, peeled and chopped
milk 750ml (1¼ pints)
vegetable stock cube 1, crumbled
nutmeg ½ tsp
celery salt a pinch
freshly ground black pepper

Melt the butter in a large saucepan over a medium heat. Add the cauliflower florets and onion and cook for 2 minutes. Then add the milk, stock cube, nutmeg, celery salt and season with pepper.

Cover and bring to the boil. Then reduce the heat and simmer for 10 minutes. Remove the pan from the heat and purée the soup using a hand-held stick blender.

Curried Spinach & Cauliflower Soup Ⓥ Ⓕ

Time 30 mins. Per portion: 206 Kcal
9g fat (3.5g saturated). Serves 4

butter 25g (1oz)
onion 1, peeled and chopped
curry paste 1 tbsp
cauliflower 1 large, broken into florets
potato 1 large, peeled and chopped
vegetable stock 900ml (1½ pints)
spinach 225g (8oz)

Melt the butter in a saucepan over a medium heat. Add the onion for cook for about 4 minutes until softened. Add the curry paste and fry for a further minute.

Stir in the cauliflower and potato. Pour in the stock and then simmer for 15 minutes or until vegetables are tender.

Remove from the heat and purée the soup using a hand-held stick blender. Add the spinach and heat through until it has wilted.

Mushroom, Cranberry & Chestnut Soup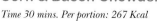

Time 30 mins. Per portion: 199 Kcal
8g fat (3.7g saturated). Serves 4

butter 25g
onion 1, peeled and chopped
garlic 1 clove, peeled and crushed
mixed mushrooms 150g (5oz), wiped and sliced
chestnut purée 435g can
vegetable stock 1 litre (1¾ pints)
chopped thyme 1 tbsp
salt and freshly ground black pepper

Melt the butter in a saucepan over a medium heat. Add the onion and garlic and cook for about 4 minutes until softened. Add the mushrooms and cook for 3–4 minutes.

Mix the chestnut purée into the pan, vegetable stock and thyme and bring to the boil. Cover and simmer for 15 minutes. Remove from the heat and purée the soup using a hand-held stick blender. Season to taste and serve.

Corn & Bacon Chowder

Time 30 mins. Per portion: 267 Kcal
8g fat (3g saturated). Serves 4

streaky bacon 75g (3oz), chopped
onion 1, peeled and chopped
potatoes 450g (1lb), peeled and diced
frozen sweetcorn 225g (8oz)
chicken stock 450ml (¾ pint)
milk 450ml (¾ pint)

Fry the bacon in a saucepan for 2 minutes over a medium heat. Drain well, then add the onion, potatoes, sweetcorn and stock. Cover and bring to the boil, then reduce the heat and simmer for 15 minutes.

Remove from the heat and purée the soup using a hand-held stick blender. Add the milk, reheat gently and serve.

Minted Pea & Bacon Soup

Time 25 mins. Per portion: 210 Kcal
14g fat (6.4g saturated). Serves 6

butter 15g (½oz)
olive oil 1 tbsp
smoked bacon rashers 150g (5oz), chopped
onion 1 large, peeled and chopped
frozen peas 400g (14oz)
vegetable stock 1.3 litres (2½ pints)
mint several sprigs, leaves chopped
single cream 150ml (¼ pint)

Melt the butter with the oil in a large saucepan over a medium heat. Add the bacon and onion and fry for 5 minutes.

Add the peas and stock, cover and bring to the boil. Then reduce the heat and simmer for 10 minutes. Stir in the mint, remove the pan from the heat and purée the soup using a hand-held stick blender. Add the cream, reheat gently without boiling and serve.

Bacon, Leek & Potato Soup

Time 30 mins. Per portion: 279 Kcal
19g fat (10.1g saturated). Serves 2

butter 25g (1oz)
onion 1 small, peeled and chopped
leek 1 small, trimmed and sliced
streaky bacon 4 rashers, chopped
potato 1, peeled and cubed
ham or vegetable stock 300ml (½ pint)
milk 150ml (¼ pint)

Melt the butter in a saucepan over a medium heat. Add the onion and leek and cook for about 4 minutes until softened. Add the bacon and cook for 2–3 minutes. Add the potato and cook for 1–2 minutes.

Pour in the stock, cover and bring to the boil. Then reduce the heat and simmer for 12–15 minutes until the potato is tender.

Remove from the heat and purée the soup using a hand-held stick blender. Add the milk and then reheat gently before serving.

Tomato & Corn Soup Ⓥ Ⓕ

Time 50 mins. Per portion: 178 Kcal
9g fat (3.7g saturated). Serves 4

corn on the cob 2
butter 25g (1oz)
olive oil 1 tbsp
onion 1 large, peeled and finely chopped
green pepper 1, deseeded and thinly sliced
red pepper 1, deseeded and thinly sliced
chopped tomatoes 400g can
vegetable stock 750ml (1¼ pints)
salt and freshly ground black pepper

Holding onto it firmly, hold one cob of corn upright on a board, with its wider end down. Then, with a sharp knife and cutting from top to bottom, very carefully cut off the kernels. Repeat with the other cob.

Heat the butter and oil in a large saucepan over a medium heat. Add the onion, red and green peppers and cook for about 4 minutes until softened.

Add the sweetcorn kernels, chopped tomatoes and vegetable stock, cover and bring to the boil. Then reduce the heat and simmer for 30–40 minutes until the vegetables are cooked through. Season with salt and pepper to taste if you like and serve soup immediately.

Roast Tomato Soup Ⓥ Ⓕ

Time 1 hr. Per portion: 98 Kcal
5g fat (0.6g saturated). Serves 6

plum tomatoes 1.3kg (3lb), halved
garlic 1 whole bulb, cut in half horizontally
oregano a few large sprigs
thyme a few large sprigs
shallots 2, peeled and finely chopped
salt 1 tsp
soft brown sugar 1 tsp
olive oil 2 tbsp
salt and freshly ground black pepper
vegetable stock 900ml (1½ pints)
sun-dried tomato paste 1 tbsp

Preheat the oven to 200°C/400°F/Gas 6. Place the plum tomato and garlic halves, cut-side up, in a large roasting pan. Add the oregano and thyme sprigs, shallots, salt, sugar and olive oil and plenty of black pepper. Bake in the oven for 30–35 minutes or until the tomatoes are soft.

Carefully squeeze the garlic pulp from their papery skins and return to the tomatoes. Stir in the stock and tomato paste, then place the pan on the hob and bring to the boil. Simmer for 5 minutes.

Remove the herbs and then remove the pan from the heat and purée the soup using a hand-held stick blender. Season with salt and pepper to taste and serve.

Carrot & Tomato Soup Ⓥ Ⓕ

Time 45 mins. Per portion: 130 Kcal
5g fat (0.6g saturated). Serves 6

olive oil 2 tbsp
onions 2 large, peeled and chopped
carrots 680g (1½lb), peeled and sliced
medium curry powder 1½–2 tbsp
chopped tomatoes 400g can
vegetable stock 1½ litres (2½ pints)
salt and freshly ground black pepper

Heat the oil in a large saucepan over a medium heat. Add the onions and cook for about 4 minutes until softened, taking care not to let them brown.

Add the carrots, curry powder, tomatoes and stock. Cover and bring to the boil, then reduce the heat and simmer for 25–30 minutes until the vegetables are softened.

Remove the pan from the heat and purée the soup using a hand-held stick blender. Season to taste and serve.

10

Pumpkin Soup Ⓥ Ⓕ

Time 45 mins. Per portion: 127 Kcal
3g fat (1.5g saturated). Serves 4

pumpkin 900g (2lb) peeled, deseeded and chopped
onion 1, peeled and chopped
turmeric ½ tsp
canned chopped tomatoes 110g (4oz)
caster sugar 1 tsp
grated nutmeg a pinch
milk 600ml (1 pint)
cornflour 2 tsp
low fat natural yogurt 1 tbsp

Place the pumpkin, onion, turmeric, tomatoes, sugar, nutmeg and milk in a large saucepan. Cover with a lid and bring to the boil, then reduce the heat and simmer for 15–20 minutes. Remove the pan from the heat and purée the soup using a hand-held stick blender.

Blend the cornflour and yogurt and add to the soup. Bring back up to simmering point, but do not boil, and serve.

Parsnip & Carrot Soup Ⓥ Ⓕ

Time 40 mins. Per portion: 242 Kcal
9g fat (2.5g saturated). Serves 4

onion 1, peeled and chopped
parsnips 350g (12oz), peeled and diced
carrots 350g (12oz), peeled and diced
vegetable stock 600ml (1 pint)
peanut butter 3 tbsp
milk 600ml (1 pint)
salt and freshly ground black pepper

Place the vegetables in a large saucepan with the stock and peanut butter. Cover and bring to the boil, then reduce the heat and simmer for 15 minutes.

Remove the pan from the heat and roughly purée the soup using a hand-held stick blender. Add the milk and season to taste. Reheat the soup gently and serve.

Coconut Soup Ⓥ Ⓕ

Time 1 hr. Per portion: 211 Kcal
12g fat (7.8g saturated). Serves 4

butter 25g (1oz)
onion 1 large, peeled and sliced
plain flour 15g (½oz)
milk 750ml (1¼ pints)
desiccated coconut 2 tbsp
eating apple 1, peeled, cored and sliced
salt and freshly ground black pepper

Melt the butter in a large saucepan over a medium heat. Add the onion and cook for about 4 minutes until softened. Stir in the flour and cook for 1 minute.

Gradually stir in the milk and coconut and bring to the boil, stirring. Add the apple, cover and simmer for 30 minutes. Remove from the heat and purée using a hand-held stick blender. Season to taste and serve.

Spring Vegetable Soup Ⓥ Ⓕ

Time 1 hr. Per portion: 77 Kcal
4g fat (2.2g saturated). Serves 6

butter 25g (1oz)
baby corn 75g (3oz), thinly sliced
baby carrots 110g (4oz), thinly sliced
fine green beans 110g (4oz), chopped
baby leeks 110g (4oz), trimmed and thinly sliced
spring onions 4, trimmed and thinly sliced
vegetable stock 1.25 litres (2 pints)
lemon thyme 4 sprigs
chopped parsley 2 tbsp
frozen peas 110g (4oz)
salt and freshly ground black pepper

Melt the butter in a large saucepan over a medium heat. Add all the vegetables except the peas and cook for 5 minutes.

Add the stock and herbs, cover and bring to the boil. Simmer for 30–40 minutes until the vegetables are soft. Add the peas and cook for 5 minutes. Season to taste and serve.

Red Bean & Squash Soup Ⓥ Ⓕ

Time 40 mins. Per portion: 227 Kcal
7g fat (0.7g saturated). Serves 4

vegetable oil 2 tbsp
butternut squash 1kg (2lb 4oz), peeled,
deseeded and chopped
chopped thyme 1 tbsp
dried chilli flakes ½ tsp
ground coriander 2 tsp
red onion 1 large, peeled and chopped
soft brown sugar 2 tsp
vegetable stock 750ml (1¼ pints)
red kidney beans 400g can, rinsed and drained
salt and freshly ground black pepper

Heat the oil in a large saucepan over a
medium heat. Add the butternut squash,
thyme, chilli flakes, coriander and onion and
fry for 5 minutes, stirring. **Add the sugar**
and stock, cover and bring to the boil. Then
reduce the heat and simmer for 10–15
minutes until the squash is tender.

Stir in the beans and cook for 2 minutes.
Using a potato masher, pulp the soup lightly
until the squash and beans are broken up
but still chunky. Season with salt and pepper
to taste and serve.

Mexican Bean Soup Ⓕ

Time 35 mins. Per portion: 150 Kcal
4g fat (2.2g saturated). Serves 6

butter 25g (1oz)
red onion 1, peeled and finely chopped
garlic 2 cloves, peeled and crushed
ground cumin 1 tsp
ground coriander 1 tsp
dried chilli flakes ½ tsp
vegetable stock 900ml (1½ pints)
chopped tomatoes 400g can
red kidney beans 2 x 400g cans, rinsed
and drained
Worcestershire sauce 1 tbsp
salt and freshly ground black pepper

Melt the butter in a large saucepan over a
medium heat. Add the onion and garlic and
cook for about 4 minutes until softened. Add
the cumin, coriander and chilli flakes and
cook for a further 1–2 minutes.

Pour in the vegetable stock, chopped
tomatoes and kidney beans. Cover and bring
to the boil, then reduce the heat and simmer
for 15 minutes until the beans and other
vegetables are cooked.

Remove the pan from the heat and
purée the soup using a hand-held stick
blender. Add the Worcestershire sauce and
season with salt and pepper to taste. Serve
immediately.

Mushroom Soup Ⓥ Ⓕ

Time 55 mins plus soaking. Per portion: 118 Kcal
8.5g fat (4.2g saturated). Serves 4

butter 25g (1oz)
onion 1 large, peeled and finely chopped
dried porcini mushrooms 15g (½oz), soaked in
250ml (8fl oz) boiling water for 20-30 minutes
large, flat mushrooms 400g (14oz) wiped, and
chopped
vegetable stock 600ml (1 pint)
milk 500ml (18fl oz)
lemon 1, juice only
salt and freshly ground black pepper

Melt the butter in a large saucepan over a
medium heat. Add the onion and cook for
about 4 minutes until softened.

Strain the liquid from the porcini through
a sheet of kitchen paper. Add the liquid with
all mushrooms to the pan, then stir in the
stock and milk, cover and bring to the boil.
Reduce the heat and simmer for 30 minutes.

Remove the pan from the heat and purée
the soup using a hand-held stick blender.
Season with salt and pepper, and add lemon
juice to taste and serve.

Lentil Soup Ⓥ Ⓕ

Time 1 hr. Per portion: 176 Kcal
6g fat (3.3g saturated). Serves 4

butter 25g (1oz)
onion 1 large, peeled and chopped
carrot 1 large, peeled and chopped
split red lentils 110g (4oz)
medium curry paste 2 tsp
vegetable stock 600ml (1 pint)
chopped tomatoes ½ 400g can
salt and freshly ground black pepper

Melt the butter in a large saucepan over a
medium heat. Add the onion and carrot and
cook gently for 10 minutes until softened.

Stir in the lentils and curry paste, then add
the stock and tomatoes. Cover and bring to
the boil. Then reduce the heat and simmer
for about 40 minutes until the lentils are soft.

Remove from the heat and purée the soup
using a hand-held stick blender. Season with
salt and pepper to taste and serve.

Cock-a-Leekie Soup

Time 1½ hrs. Per portion: 176 Kcal
5g fat (2.3g saturated). Serves 4

unsalted butter 15g (½oz)
skinless chicken breasts 350g (12oz)
leeks 350g (12oz), trimmed and sliced
chicken stock 1.25 litres (2 pints)
bouquet garni 1
salt and freshly ground black pepper
ready to eat prunes 8, stoned and halved

Melt the butter in a large saucepan and fry
the chicken for 4-5 minutes, until golden on
all sides. Add the leeks to the pan and fry for
2-3 minutes until softened.

Add the stock and herbs and season. Bring
to the boil and simmer for 30 minutes. Add
the prunes and cook for 35 minutes.

To serve, cut the chicken into pieces and
place in warmed bowls with the soup.

Chicken Noodle Soup

Time 35 mins. Per portion: 555 Kcal
24g fat (16.2g saturated). Serves 4

vegetable oil 1 tbsp
shallots 4, peeled and sliced
chestnut mushrooms 110g (4oz), wiped
and sliced
Thai red curry paste 1 tbsp
chicken stock 1.3 litres (2¼ pints)
coconut cream 200ml (7fl oz)
medium egg thread noodles 4 portions
cooked skinless chicken breasts 2, shredded
soy sauce to taste

Heat the oil in a large saucepan over a
medium heat. Add the shallots and cook
for 2–3 minutes until softened. Add the
mushrooms and cook for 3–4 minutes.

Stir in the curry paste and fry for 2–3
minutes, then add the stock and coconut
cream. Cover and bring to the boil, then
reduce the heat and simmer for 4–5 minutes.

Add the noodles and simmer for 3 minutes.
Stir in the chicken, season with soy sauce
and serve when the chicken is hot.

Turkey Soup Ⓩ

Time 3 hrs. Per portion: 213 Kcal
9g fat (4.3g saturated). Serves 4

turkey carcass 1
onions 2 large, peeled and chopped
carrots 3 large, peeled and sliced
chopped parsley 2–3 tbsp
black peppercorns 2 tsp
butter 25g (1oz)
potato 1 large, peeled and diced
leek 1, trimmed and thinly sliced
cooked turkey meat 150g (5oz), chopped
cooked gammon or ham 150g (5oz), diced
salt and freshly ground black pepper

Cut up the turkey carcass and place it in a large saucepan. Barely cover with water and bring up to the boil.

Add the onions, carrots, parsley and peppercorns to the pan, cover and cook gently for 2–3 hours. Allow to cool, then strain and reserve the stock.

Heat the butter in a large saucepan over a medium heat. Add the potato and leek and cook gently for 10 minutes.

Add 1 litre (1¾ pints) of the turkey stock and cook gently for 45 minutes. Then add the chopped turkey and diced gammon or ham. Heat through for 10–15 minutes until the meat is hot, season with salt and pepper to taste, then serve.

Spicy Split Pea & Ham Soup

Time 1 hr plus soaking. Per portion: 379 Kcal
10g fat (4.6g saturated). Serves 4

butter 25g (1oz)
onion 1, peeled and chopped
garlic 1, peeled and crushed
ground cumin 1 tsp
ground coriander 2 tsp
ground turmeric ½ tsp
split peas 250g (9oz), soaked as packet's instructions

vegetable stock 1 litre (1¾ pints)
chopped tomatoes 400g can
ham 250g (9oz), cubed
salt and freshly ground black pepper

Melt the butter in a saucepan over a medium heat. Add the onion and garlic and cook for about 4 minutes until softened. Add the spices and cook for a further minute.

Stir in the peas, stock and tomatoes, cover and bring to the boil. Then simmer for 45 minutes. Remove from the heat and purée using a hand-held stick blender. Stir in the cubed ham, season to taste and serve.

Speedy Bortsch

Time 45 mins. Per portion: 207 Kcal
6g fat (3.3g saturated). Serves 4

butter 25g (1oz)
onion 1 large, peeled and finely chopped
carrot 1 large, peeled and coarsely grated
parsnip 1 large, peeled and coarsely grated
beef or chicken stock 1.3 litres (2¼ pints)
savoy cabbage 150g (5oz), very finely shredded
cooked, peeled beetroot 500g (1lb 2oz), coarsely grated
Frankfurter sausages 250g (9oz) sliced
lemon 1, juice only
chopped parsley 2 tbsp
salt and freshly ground black pepper

Melt the butter in a large saucepan over a medium heat. Add the onion, carrot and parsnip and cook for 5 minutes.

Add the stock to pan, cover with a lid and bring to boil. Then reduce the heat and simmer for 20–25 minutes until the vegetables are tender.

Stir the cabbage and beetroot into the soup together with the Frankfurters. Continue cooking for about 5 minutes until the cabbage is tender. Stir in the lemon juice and parsley, season with salt and pepper to taste and serve.

Vegetable & Chorizo Soup

Time 1 hr. Per portion: 296 Kcal
13g fat (3.4g saturated). Serves 4

olive oil 2 tbsp
onion 1 large, peeled and finely chopped
garlic 1–2 cloves, peeled and crushed
potato 1 large, peeled and diced
carrots 2 large, peeled and diced
courgette 1 large, sliced
green cabbage 200g (7oz), finely shredded
chopped tomatoes 400g can
dried mixed herbs or oregano 2 tsp
vegetable stock 1.25 litres (2 pints)
small pasta shapes 50g (2oz)
chorizo sausage 110–150g (4–5oz), thinly sliced
salt and freshly ground black pepper

Heat the oil in a very large saucepan over a medium heat. Add the onion, garlic, potato and carrots and cook for about 5 minutes, stirring frequently.

Add the courgette, cabbage, tomatoes, herbs and stock. Cover and bring to the boil. Then reduce the heat and simmer for 30–40 minutes until the vegetables are softened, but not broken up.

Add the pasta shapes and sliced chorizo and continue cooking for 5–6 minutes, until the pasta is cooked, but slightly firm. Season with salt and pepper to taste, if necessary, and serve.

Chorizo & Kale Soup

Time 40 mins. Per portion: 202 Kcal
14g fat (6.9g saturated). Serves 3

butter 25g (1oz)
onion 1, peeled and chopped
chorizo sausage 75g (3oz), sliced
potato 1 large, peeled and cubed
garlic 1clove, peeled and crushed
ham or vegetable stock 600ml (1 pint)
kale 50g (2oz), finely shredded
salt and freshly ground black pepper

Melt the butter in a large saucepan over a medium heat. Add the onion and cook for about 4 minutes until softened. Then add the chorizo, potato and garlic and cook for a further 1-2 minutes.

Pour the stock into the pan and bring to the boil. Then reduce the heat, cover and simmer for 12-15 minutes or until the potato is tender. Use a potato masher to mash some of the potato and thicken the soup.

Add the kale and then simmer, uncovered for 2-3 minutes, until the kale has wilted and is tender. Season with salt and pepper to taste and serve.

SALADS & SANDWICHES

QUICK & EASY

Salad Panzanella

Time required 20 mins. Per portion: 175 Kcal, 9g fat (1.2g saturated)

Serves 6-8

crusty baton bread (preferably a day old) 250g (9oz), thickly sliced and torn into small chunks

olive oil 6 tbsp, plus extra to taste

red or white wine vinegar 2 tbsp, plus extra to taste

cucumber 1, peeled and cut into 2.5cm (1in) chunks

red onion 1, peeled and finely chopped

garlic 2 cloves, peeled and finely chopped

tomatoes 8–10, halved and roughly chopped

salt and freshly ground black pepper

basil leaves a handful, torn

ready-to-eat cold meat or fish (if not vegetarian) to serve, optional

QR Code
Scan with a smartphone for an ingredients shopping list.

Tip the chunks of bread into a bowl and add all the other ingredients except for the seasoning and basil. Cover and leave to stand for 10 minutes for the flavours to infuse.

Mix well with your hands, taste and add a little more oil and vinegar if necessary.

Season with salt and pepper and scatter with basil leaves. Serve immediately with a selection of barbecued meats or fish or ready-to-eat cold Italian meats (if not serving vegetarians).

19

Pear & Stilton Salad

Time required 5 mins. Per portion: 493 Kcal, 39g fat (11.4g saturated)

Serves 2

Put the prepared salad and chicory leaves in a bowl. Add the pears to the bowl with the Stilton followed by the walnut pieces. Drizzle with the oil and lime juice, mix gently and season with salt and pepper.

Arrange the salad neatly in the centre of two large plates and serve at once with a warmed par-baked roll per person.

mixed leaf salad 50g (2oz)

chicory 1 head, halved, leaves separated and torn into large pieces

conference pears 2, cored and sliced

Stilton cheese 75g (3oz), crumbled

walnut pieces 25g (1oz)

walnut oil 1 tbsp

extra virgin olive oil 2 tbsp

lime 1, juice only

salt and freshly ground black pepper

par-baked rolls 2, warmed, to serve, optional

QR Code
Scan with a smartphone for an ingredients shopping list.

20

Tabbouleh with Chickpeas

Time required 25 mins. Per portion: 188 Kcal, 10g fat (1.3g saturated)

Serves 6

bulgar wheat 90g (3½oz)

lemon juice 2 tbsp

extra virgin olive oil 4 tbsp

finely chopped parsley 5 tbsp

finely chopped mint leaves 5 tbsp

finely chopped dill 2 tbsp

cherry tomatoes 250g (9oz), halved

chickpeas 400g can, drained and rinsed

mixed salad leaves 110–150g (4–5oz)

salt and freshly ground black pepper

pitta bread toasted, to serve, optional

QR Code
Scan with a smartphone for an ingredients shopping list.

Put the bulgar wheat in a heatproof bowl and pour over 400ml (14fl oz) boiling water. Stir, cover tightly with cling film and set aside for 8–10 minutes (stir once halfway through).

Put the lemon juice and oil in a small bowl and whisk. Drain any excess water from the bulgar wheat then pour the oil and lemon juice over the bulgar and stir well with a fork, fluffing up the bulgar and separating the grains.

Add the parsley, mint, dill, tomatoes, chickpeas and salad leaves to the bulgar and use your hands to toss everything together. Season well with salt and pepper, then transfer to a serving plate and serve with toasted pitta, if you like.

23

Grilled Goat's Cheese Salad

Time required 15 mins. Per portion: 500 Kcal, 34.5g fat (19.9g saturated)

Serves 4

Slice the tops and bottoms from the oranges. Using a small, sharp knife, slice off the skin taking away as much of the pith as possible. Holding each orange over a bowl, slice in between the segments to release the flesh and juice into the bowl.

Preheat the grill to a hot setting. Line the grill tray with foil. Place the cheese on the foil. Cook under the grill for about 2 minutes until lightly golden and slightly melting.

Arrange the salad leaves on four serving plates. Drain the orange segments, reserving the juice, and arrange over the leaves, then sprinkle the beetroot on top. Top the salad with the goat's cheese, cut in half if preferred.

Blend the mustard, honey and oil with the orange juice. Season the dressing and spoon over the salad. Serve immediately.

oranges 4 large

firm goat's cheese 4 x 110g (4oz) pieces

bistro salad 150g bag of lamb's lettuce, baby red chard and beetroot strips

cooked beetroot in natural juice 200g pack, drained and cut into thin batons

wholegrain mustard 1 tbsp

clear honey 1 tsp

olive oil 2 tbsp

salt and freshly ground black pepper

QR Code
Scan with a smartphone for an ingredients shopping list.

Soft goat's cheese melts in the mouth in
this delicious crisp and tangy salad.

*A hearty and healthy taste of Italy, which
is simple to prepare yet delicious.*

Italian Tuna & Beans

Time required 20 mins. Per portion: 292 Kcal, 14g fat (2.1g saturated)

Serves 4-6

tuna steak 1 large, about 250g (9oz), or 2 x 160g cans tuna, drained

olive oil 6 tbsp, plus extra for brushing

garlic 2–3 large cloves, peeled and crushed

sherry vinegar or white wine vinegar 1 tbsp

red onions 2, peeled and finely sliced

green flageolet beans or white cannellini beans (or a mixture of both) 3 x 400g cans, drained and rinsed

basil leaves 4 handfuls

salt and freshly ground black pepper

crusty bread to serve, optional

QR Code
Scan with a smartphone for an ingredients shopping list.

If using fresh tuna, brush with olive oil and put it onto a preheated griddle. Cook for 3 minutes on each side or until barred with brown but pink in the middle (the cooking time will depend on the thickness of the fish). Remove from the pan, cool and cut into chunks.

Put the oil, garlic and vinegar in a bowl and beat with a fork. Add the onions and beans and toss until well coated.

Add the tuna and basil leaves, and salt and pepper to taste. Serve with crusty bread.

27

Mackerel & Bulgar Wheat Salad

Time required 20 mins. Per portion: 425 Kcal, 26g fat (6.8g saturated)

Serves 2

Put the bulgar wheat in a heatproof bowl and add 125ml (4fl oz) boiling water. Stir once, cover tightly with cling film and set aside for 8–10 minutes. Drain, then stir in the lemon juice, chives, yellow pepper and radishes.

Put the spinach leaves into shallow individual salad bowls, spoon the bulgar wheat on top, then add the flaked smoked mackerel.

Mix the dressing ingredients together in a bowl and drizzle over the fish.

bulgar wheat 60g (2½oz)

lemon juice 1 tbsp

finely snipped chives 1 tbsp

yellow pepper ½, deseeded and diced

radishes 8, trimmed and sliced

spinach leaves 75g (3oz)

smoked mackerel fillets 150g (5oz), flaked

for the dressing

fromage frais 3 tbsp

horseradish sauce 2 tsp

finely snipped chives 1 tsp

freshly ground black pepper

QR Code
Scan with a smartphone for an ingredients shopping list.

Looking for lunchbox inspiration?
These wraps are packed full of flavour.

Creamy Prawn Wraps

Time required 10 mins. Per portion: 310 Kcal, 11g fat (4.1g saturated)

Serves 4

light soft cream cheese 200g (7oz)

snipped chives 3 tbsp

peeled prawns 175g (6oz), thawed if frozen

Tabasco sauce to taste, optional

tortillas 4

large plum tomatoes 3, quartered and cut into thin strips lengthways

rocket leaves 50g (2oz)

watercress 50g (2oz)

QR Code
Scan with a Smartphone for an ingredients shopping list

Put the cream cheese into a bowl and beat with a fork until softened. Add the chives and prawns, season with Tabasco sauce if you like (3–4 drops) and then mix together gently.

Dividing the cheese mixture evenly, spread it over each tortilla. Then sprinkle each one equally with the tomato strips.

Scatter the rocket leaves and watercress over the tomatoes, and then roll up each tortilla tightly.

31

Chicken Fajita

Time required 25 mins. Per portion: 450 Kcal, 17g fat (4.3g saturated)

Serves 4

Tip 2 tablespoons of the oil into a bowl, add the strips of chicken and fajita seasoning and stir until the chicken is well coated.

Heat the remaining oil in a large frying pan over a medium heat. Add the chicken and stir-fry for 5–8 minutes until the chicken is beginning to cook through. Then add the pepper and spring onions and cook for a further 3–5 minutes or until the chicken is cooked.

Put each warmed tortilla on a plate. Spread each one with 1 tablespoon of cream or yogurt, then add a portion of salad leaves and a portion of chicken. Roll tightly, cut in half, and serve.

- **sunflower oil** 3 tbsp
- **skinless chicken breast fillets** 4, cut into fine strips
- **fajita seasoning mix** 1-2 tbsp
- **red pepper** 1 large, deseeded and cut into fine strips
- **spring onions** 4, trimmed and sliced
- **plain tortilla wraps** 4, warmed according to the packet's instructions
- **sour cream or plain Greek yogurt** 4 tbsp
- **mixed salad** 50g (2oz)

QR Code
Scan with a smartphone for an ingredients shopping list.

Curried Chicken
with Garlic Naans

Time required 30 mins. Per portion: 831 Kcal, 30g fat (13.6g saturated)

Serves 2

olive oil 1–2 tbsp

onion 1, peeled and chopped

skinless chicken breast fillets 2, diced

korma curry paste 1–3 tsp

double cream 4 tbsp

mango 1 peeled, stoned and diced

garlic and coriander naans 2, warmed according to the packet's instructions

chopped coriander 2 tbsp

tomato and red onion salad to serve, optional

QR Code
Scan with a smartphone for an ingredients shopping list.

Heat 1 tablespoon of oil in a large frying pan over a medium heat. Add the onion and cook for about 5 minutes until softened. Then add the chicken, and more oil if necessary, and continue cooking for a further 5 minutes, stirring often.

Stir in curry paste to taste plus 4 tablespoons of water and continue cooking for a further 5 minutes, still stirring. Then add the cream and continue cooking until the sauce has thickened and the chicken is cooked. Remove the pan from the heat and cool quickly.

Stir in the mango and then spoon the chicken mixture onto the warmed naans, scatter with the coriander and serve immediately with a salad.

Crunchy Bacon Salad

Time required 20 mins. Per portion: 347 Kcal, 26g fat (6.7g saturated)

Serves 2

Heat the oil in a large frying pan over a medium heat. Add the bacon and cook for 5 minutes, stirring frequently. Then add the focaccia and continue cooking over a medium heat for about 5 minutes until the bread is crispy. Stir in the garlic for the last few minutes.

Arrange the prepared salad leaves on two plates, then scatter with the hot garlicky bacon and croutons. Drizzle with a little extra oil and lime juice, to taste, and season with salt and pepper. Serve immediately topped with shavings of Parmesan cheese.

extra virgin olive oil 1 tbsp, plus extra for drizzling to taste

bacon lardons 110g (4oz)

focaccia 75g (3oz), cubed

garlic 2 cloves, peeled and finely chopped

mixed salad leaves 50g (2oz)

lime 1, juice only

salt and freshly ground black pepper

Parmesan shavings to serve, optional

QR Code
Scan with a smartphone for an ingredients shopping list.

Steak Ciabatta with Caramelised Onions

Time required 25 mins. Per portion: 523 Kcal, 19g fat (6.4g saturated)

Serves 2

butter 15g (½oz)

olive oil 1–2 tbsp

red onions 2, peeled and sliced

balsamic vinegar 1 tsp

rump steak 400g (14oz), trimmed and cut into fine strips

steak seasoning 2 tsp, optional

Italian-style ciabatta rolls 2, warmed according to the packet's instructions

rocket leaves 15g (½oz)

mayonnaise to serve, optional

QR Code
Scan with a smartphone for an ingredients shopping list.

Heat the butter and 1 tablespoon of the oil in a large frying pan over a medium-low heat. Add the onions and cook for 5–10 minutes until softened and beginning to colour. Stir in the vinegar and cook, stirring frequently, until the onions are evenly glazed. Remove from the pan and set aside.

Increase the heat to medium-high. Toss the strips of steak in the steak seasoning (if using) and add to the frying pan with the remaining oil. Stir-fry to taste – it will not take long – turning and stirring frequently.

Cut the warm ciabattas in half and spoon the caramelised onions onto the bread, top with the stir-fried steak and scatter with rocket leaves. Serve with a generous dollop of mayonnaise, if wished.

39

QUICK & EASY

MAIN COURSES

TAKE IT EASY

Greek-Style Omelette

Time required 25 mins. Per portion: 462 Kcal, 40g fat (10.9g saturated)

Serves 3

olive oil for frying

cherry tomatoes 110g (4oz), halved

bottled hot yellow peppers 4–5, drained and sliced

spring onions 3, trimmed and sliced

pitted black olives 40g (2½oz), sliced

feta cheese 110g (4oz)

salt and freshly ground black pepper

chopped flat-leaf parsley a small handful

eggs 6 large

for the salad

crispy mixed salad 200g (7oz)

lemon juice 1 tbsp

extra virgin olive oil 4 tbsp

QR Code
Scan with a smartphone for an ingredients shopping list.

Preheat the oven to 200°C/400°F/Gas 6.

Rub a deep ovenproof frying pan with olive oil, then arrange the tomatoes, hot peppers, spring onions and olives equally around it. Crumble in the feta cheese, then grind pepper over the top and sprinkle with the parsley.

Put the eggs in a bowl, season with a good pinch of salt and beat well. Pour over the ingredients in the pan. Bake in the preheated oven for 15–20 minutes until puffed and just golden around the edges.

To make the salad, put the leaves in a bowl, add the lemon juice and oil and season with salt and pepper. Toss well, then taste and adjust the seasoning with more salt and pepper if necessary. Serve with the omelette cut into wedges – hot, warm or at room temperature.

Sun-Dried Tomato Frittata

Time required 15 mins. Per portion: 272 Kcal, 19g fat (4.9g saturated)

Serves 2-3

Preheat the grill to hot. Break the eggs into a large bowl and whisk briefly with a fork. Add the sun-dried tomatoes, sage, olives and Parmesan cheese (or a vegetarian version). Mix together gently and season with salt and pepper.

Heat the oil in a large non-stick frying pan over a medium heat. Add the onion and cook for about 5 minutes until softened and golden. Pour the egg mixture into the pan and stir just long enough to mix in the onion. Cook over a medium-low heat until the base of the frittata is golden and the top has almost set.

Slide the pan under the grill to finish cooking or put a plate on top of the pan and invert the pan so the frittata drops onto the plate. Return the frittata to the pan, cooked-side up, and cook on top of the stove for 1–2 minutes.

Transfer the frittata to a serving plate and serve hot or cold, cut into wedges with a tomato salad.

eggs 6 large

sun-dried tomatoes in oil 8, drained and sliced

chopped sage 1 tbsp

pitted black olives 50g (2oz), thickly sliced

Parmesan-style hard cheese 50g (2oz), grated

salt and freshly ground black pepper

olive oil 2 tbsp

onion 1, peeled and sliced

tomato salad to serve, optional

QR Code
Scan with a smartphone for an ingredients shopping list.

44

Spiced Mixed Vegetables

Time required 25 mins. Per portion: 170 Kcal, 8g fat (0.8g saturated)

Serves 2

grated fresh ginger 1 tsp

garlic 2 cloves, peeled and chopped

vegetable oil 1 tbsp

fennel seeds ½ tsp

cumin seeds 1 tsp

onion 1, peeled and sliced

ground cumin ¼ tsp

ground coriander ¼ tsp

chilli powder ½ tsp

canned chopped tomatoes 150g (5oz)

cauliflower 200g (7oz), cut into small florets

carrots 110g (4oz), peeled and cut into batons

green beans 110g (4oz), sliced on the diagonal into 3cm (1¼in) pieces

salt

chopped coriander 2 tbsp

cooked microwave basmati rice 250g packet to serve, optional

QR Code
Scan with a smartphone for an ingredients shopping list.

Place the ginger and garlic in a pestle and mortar and grind to a paste.

Heat the oil in a lidded wok or large frying pan, add the fennel and cumin seeds and stir until they start to pop. Add the onion and cook for a further 3–4 minutes until golden. Stir in the ginger and garlic paste and continue to cook for a further 2 minutes, stirring. Spoon in the ground cumin, ground coriander and chilli powder and, after a few seconds, the tomatoes. Cook briskly for 1 minute until most of the liquid has evaporated.

Add the cauliflower and carrots to the wok with a good sprinkle of water, stir, then cover immediately and cook for 2 minutes.

Add the green beans, season with salt and cook for a further 2–3 minutes until the vegetables are cooked but still a little crunchy. Taste and add more salt if necessary. Remove from the heat and stir in the coriander leaves. Serve immediately with rice.

47

Mustardy Mushroom Stroganoff

Time required 20 mins. Per portion: 118 Kcal, 7.5g fat (4g saturated)

Serves 1

Put 3 tablespoons of the stock in a saucepan over a medium heat, add the onion and cover with a lid. Cook for about 4 minutes or until the onion has softened and the liquid has evaporated.

Stir in the mushrooms and garlic and salt and pepper. Then add the remaining stock together with the mustard and tomato purée. Cover with a lid and simmer for 4 minutes, then remove the lid and cook rapidly for a further 2-5 minutes to reduce the liquid to a syrup.

Remove from the heat. Stir in the crème fraîche and parsley. Serve immediately on a bed of rice with green vegetables.

- **vegetable stock** 150ml (¼ pint)
- **onion** ½ small, peeled and sliced
- **mixed mushrooms** 150g (5oz), wiped and chopped if large
- **garlic** 1 clove, peeled and crushed
- **salt and freshly ground black pepper**
- **wholegrain mustard** 1 tsp
- **tomato purée** ½ tsp
- **crème fraîche** 1 tbsp
- **chopped parsley** to garnish, optional
- **cooked microwave wild rice** ½ 250g packet to serve, optional
- **cooked microwave green vegetables** to serve, optional

QR Code
Scan with a smartphone for an ingredients shopping list.

48

This lightly spiced curry makes
delicious cosy comfort food.

Red Kidney Bean Curry

Time required 15 mins. Per portion: 320 Kcal, 19g fat (5.4g saturated)

Serves 2

unsalted butter 15g (½oz)

sunflower oil 2 tbsp

onion 1, peeled and finely chopped

cinnamon stick 1

bay leaves 2

garlic 3 cloves, peeled and crushed

grated fresh ginger 2 tsp

ground turmeric ½ tsp

ground coriander 1 tsp

ground cumin 2 tsp

garam masala 1 tsp

dried chilli flakes ½ -1 tsp

red kidney beans 250g can, drained and rinsed

tomato purée 4 tbsp

salt

plain yogurt to drizzle, optional

chopped coriander leaves to garnish, optional

cooked microwave pilau rice 250g packet to serve, optional

Heat the butter and oil in a large heavy-based saucepan over a medium heat. Add the onion, cinnamon, bay leaves, garlic and ginger and stir-fry for 4–5 minutes until the onion has softened. Stir in the turmeric, coriander, cumin, garam masala and chilli flakes.

Add the kidney beans, tomato purée and sufficient water to make a thick sauce. Bring to the boil and cook for 4–5 minutes, stirring often. Season well with salt, then remove the cinnamon stick and bay leaves. Drizzle with yogurt, if using, and garnish with coriander before serving with rice.

51

QR Code
Scan with a smartphone for an ingredients shopping list.

Pasta with Melted Ricotta

Time required 20 mins. Per portion: 791 Kcal, 48g fat (11.3g saturated)

Serves 4

Cook the pasta according to the instructions on the packet. Drain, reserving 4 tablespoons of the cooking liquid, and return both to the pan. Add the pine nuts and oil together with the rocket, herbs, ricotta cheese, half the Parmesan cheese and plenty of salt and black pepper to taste.

Stir until the pasta is evenly coated with the sauce. Serve in warmed bowls, with the remaining Parmesan cheese sprinkled on top.

dried penne or other pasta 350g (12oz)

pine nuts 110g (4oz)

olive oil 6 tbsp

rocket leaves 70g packet, chopped

chopped parsley 2 tbsp

chopped basil 2 tbsp

ricotta cheese 250g (9oz), mashed

Parmesan-style hard cheese 50g (2oz), grated

salt and freshly ground black pepper

QR Code
Scan with a smartphone for an ingredients shopping list.

Summer Herb & Smoked Salmon Pasta

Time required 15 mins. Per portion: 515 Kcal, 14g fat (2.4g saturated)

Serves 2

fusilli pasta twists 200g (7oz)

olive oil 1 tbsp

spring onions 4, trimmed and sliced

smoked salmon 120g packet, cut into strips

lemon 1, juice only

chopped coriander 2 tbsp

chopped parsley 1 tbsp

salt and freshly ground black pepper

rocket leaves about 15g (½oz), to garnish

Cook the pasta in a large pan of salted boiling water according to the packet's instructions, which usually takes 10–12 minutes. Drain the pasta and set it aside.

Heat the olive oil in the pan over a medium heat. Add the spring onions and salmon and stir-fry the mixture for about 1 minute until the smoked salmon turns pink. Add the remaining ingredients (except the rocket), including the drained pasta and salt and pepper to taste, and mix well. Serve on warm plates, garnished with a spiral of rocket leaves.

QR Code
Scan with a smartphone for an ingredients shopping list.

Fish Molee

Time required 30 mins. Per portion: 494 Kcal, 40g fat (27.2g saturated)

Serves 4

Mix the turmeric and salt on a plate, roll the fish in the mixture and set aside for a few minutes.

Meanwhile, heat the butter in a flameproof casserole or large saucepan over a medium-low heat. Add the onion, garlic, chillies, ginger, cardamom, cloves and the cinnamon stick and fry for about 4 minutes until the onion is softened and translucent.

Add the coconut milk and heat it until the sauce is simmering then cook for 5-10 minutes until the mixture is quite thick. Add the fish to the casserole, then spoon the sauce over the top, making sure the fish is well covered. Continue simmering for about 10 minutes until the fish is opaque all the way through. Remove the cinnamon stick and serve sprinkled with lemon juice and coriander and rice, if using.

ground turmeric 1 tbsp

salt 1 tsp

firm fish such as salmon, monkfish or cod 500g (1lb 2oz), cut into 3cm (1¼in) strips

unsalted butter 110g (4oz)

onion 1, peeled and chopped

garlic 1 clove, peeled and crushed

green chillies 2 small, deseeded and chopped

fresh ginger 3cm (1¼in), peeled and grated

cardamom pods 12, crushed

cloves 6, crushed

cinnamon stick 1

coconut milk 400ml can

lemon juice to taste

torn coriander leaves to serve

cooked microwave basmati rice 2 x 250g packets to serve, optional

QR Code
Scan with a smartphone for an ingredients shopping list.

Roasted Cod Loin Wrapped in Pancetta

Time required 30 mins. Per portion: 358 Kcal, 23g fat (4.8g saturated)

Serves 2

cod loin 2 pieces, 150–175g (5–6oz) each

smoked sliced pancetta 8–10 slices, weighing about 50g (2oz)

olive oil 2 tbsp

salt and freshly ground black pepper

asparagus tips 125g (4½oz), trimmed

ready-to-eat mixed grains 250g packet (found in the couscous/rice aisle of the supermarket) to serve, optional

light mayonnaise 2–3 tbsp

lime ½–1, juice only

 QR Code
Scan with a smartphone for an ingredients shopping list.

Preheat the oven to 200°C/400°F/Gas 6. Generously wrap the cod loins in pancetta. Drizzle a little oil in a roasting tin and pop the cod loins on top of the oil. Drizzle the loins with a little more oil, season with pepper and roast in the oven for 10 minutes.

Meanwhile, tip the remaining oil into a plastic food bag. Add the asparagus tips and season with salt and pepper. Shake gently so the asparagus is lightly coated in oil.

Remove the cod loins from the oven, baste the pancetta with the juices in the pan and add the asparagus spears, making sure they are in a single layer. Roast for a further 8–10 minutes until the cod loins are cooked through and the asparagus is tender.

Heat the mixed grains (if using) in the microwave according to the packet's instructions. Flavour the mayonnaise with lime juice, adding it gradually so it doesn't split the mayonnaise, and season with salt and pepper to taste.

To serve, set a spoonful of mixed grains on each plate, pop the cod loin on top and arrange the asparagus spears neatly to the side. Serve at once with the lime mayonnaise.

Soy & Honey-Glazed Salmon with Cucumber Salad

Time required 25 mins. Per portion: 308 Kcal, 18g fat (3.6g saturated)

Serves 2

Preheat the oven to 200°C/400°F/Gas 6. Lay two sheets of tin foil measuring about 28cm (11in) square on the worksurface. Pop a salmon fillet in the centre of each sheet. Mix together the toasted sesame oil, soy sauce, ginger, lemon juice, honey and seasoning in a small bowl. Drizzle about half of the soy sauce mix over the salmon, spreading it evenly with the back of a spoon, then turn the salmon over and drizzle again with the remaining sauce. Turn the salmon back over again.

Carefully draw up the foil to cover each salmon fillet, as if making a Cornish pasty – fold down in the middle then fold the sides over to make two secure parcels. Carefully lift the parcels onto a roasting tin and bake for 10–15 minutes until the salmon is cooked through.

Meanwhile, mix together the cucumber with the spring onions and coriander.

Remove the salmon from the parcels (there will be a lot of steam, so take care), and serve with rice, spooning over any of the cooking juices. Neatly arrange the cucumber salad at the side. Serve with a little drizzle of sesame oil, soy sauce and lemon juice to taste.

skinless salmon fillets 2, about 150–175g (5–6oz) each

toasted sesame oil 1 tsp, plus extra to serve

soy sauce 2 tsp, plus extra to serve

ground ginger ½ tsp

lemon juice 1–2 tsp, plus extra to serve

runny honey 1 tsp

salt and freshly ground black pepper

cucumber ½, halved, deseeded and cut into fine matchsticks

spring onions 4, trimmed and finely chopped

chopped coriander 1–2 tbsp

cooked microwave basmati rice 250g packet to serve, optional

QR Code
Scan with a smartphone for an ingredients shopping list.

60

61

The perfect weekday dinner: nutritious,
yet quick and delicious.

Roast Salmon with Lemon & Herb Couscous

Time required 30 mins. Per portion: 441 Kcal, 29g fat (5.1g saturated)

Serves 2

lemon juice of 1

olive oil 2 tbsp

salt and freshly ground black pepper

skinless salmon fillets 2, about 150–175g (5–6oz) each

lemon, mint and parsley couscous 100g packet

rocket leaves 20g (¾oz)

light mayonnaise 2 tbsp, to serve, optional

QR Code
Scan with a smartphone for an ingredients shopping list.

To make the marinade, combine the lemon juice and 1 tablespoon of the olive oil with salt and black pepper in a bowl. Add the salmon fillets and turn the fish over twice so it is coated all over. Cover and marinate for 15 minutes.

When ready to cook, preheat the oven to 220°C/425°F/Gas 7 and drizzle the remaining oil into a small roasting tin. Drain the salmon from the marinade and pop the fish into the roasting tin. Discard the marinade. Roast for 10–15 minutes or until the salmon is starting to crisp on top and is cooked all the way through.

Meanwhile, tip the couscous into a bowl and add boiling water according to the packet's instructions. Leave the couscous to stand for about 5 minutes to absorb all the liquid and then fluff up with a fork.

Put a portion of the couscous on each plate and set a roasted salmon fillet on top. Serve with the rocket leaves and a tablespoon of mayonnaise if you like.

63

Jasmine Rice with Crab & Asparagus

Time required 20 mins. Per portion: 354 Kcal, 9g fat (1.9g saturated)

Serves 2

Heat the oil in a wok or large frying pan over a medium heat. Add the onion, increase the heat to hot and stir-fry for 2–3 minutes until the onion is softened and golden. Add the garlic and chilli and cook for a further minute. Add the asparagus stalks and stir-fry for 2 minutes, then add the tips and the soy sauce and fry for 30 seconds. Stir in the crabmeat and heat through.

Mix in the rice, then add the chilli sauce and sesame oil. Stir well until everything is thoroughly combined and the rice is piping hot. Taste and check for seasoning, adding some more soy sauce if necessary, then stir in the chives and remove from the heat. Serve immediately.

- **groundnut oil** 1 tbsp
- **onion** 1 small, peeled and finely chopped
- **garlic** 2 cloves, peeled and crushed
- **red chilli** 1 large, deseeded and finely chopped
- **fine asparagus** 125g (4½oz), cut into 2cm (¾in) pieces, tips and stalks separated
- **light soy sauce** 2 tsp, plus extra to taste
- **white crabmeat** 170g can, well drained
- **cooked jasmine rice** 250g (9oz)
- **sweet chilli sauce** 1 tbsp
- **toasted sesame oil** ¼ tsp
- **snipped chives** 2 tbsp

QR Code
Scan with a smartphone for an ingredients shopping list.

64

Chinese Lemon Chicken

Time required 30 mins. Per portion: 264 Kcal, 12g fat (2.4g saturated)

Serves 4

skinless chicken breasts 4, cut into thin strips

sesame seeds 1 tbsp

groundnut or vegetable oil 3 tbsp

onion 1, peeled and thinly sliced

spring onions 2, shredded, to garnish, optional

straight-to-wok noodles to serve, optional

for the marinade

light soy sauce 1 tbsp

Chinese rice wine or sherry 1 tbsp

grated fresh ginger 2 tsp

garlic 2 cloves, peeled and crushed

cornflour 1 tsp

for the sauce

chicken stock 90ml (3fl oz)

lemon 1, grated rind and juice

runny honey 3 tbsp

light soy sauce 1 tbsp

sesame oil 1 tsp

cornflour 2 tsp

QR Code
Scan with a smartphone for an ingredients shopping list.

To make the marinade, combine all the ingredients in a bowl. Add the chicken and mix well. Cover and marinate in the refrigerator for 10–15 minutes.

Meanwhile, to make the sauce, put all the ingredients in a bowl with 2 tablespoons of cold water, stir to combine and set aside.

Heat a wok or large frying pan over a medium heat. Add the sesame seeds and dry-fry for about 2 minutes until lightly toasted. Remove from the heat and set the seeds aside.

Heat 1½ tablespoons of the oil in the wok over a medium heat. Add half the marinated chicken and stir-fry for 3–4 minutes until it is golden brown and well sealed all over. Spoon out into a dish and repeat with the remaining chicken. Set aside.

Add ½ tablespoon of oil to the wok and add the onions. Stir-fry for 2–3 minutes until they are softened and golden. Pour in the sauce and bring to the boil, then reduce the heat and simmer for 1 minute.

Return the chicken to the wok and stir through the sauce. Simmer for 2 minutes, or until the chicken is cooked through. Remove from the pan and keep warm. Wipe the pan clean with kitchen paper and then warm the noodles with the remaining oil in the pan. Sprinkle the chicken with sesame seeds, garnish with the spring onions and serve with the noodles.

Chicken & Black Bean Stir-Fry

Time required 30 mins. Per portion: 358 Kcal, 13g fat (2.3g saturated)

Serves 2

To make the marinade, combine all the ingredients in a bowl. Add the chicken and mix well, cover and marinate in the refrigerator for 10–15 minutes.

When ready to cook, heat the oil in a wok or large frying pan over a medium heat. When hot, add the chicken and stir-fry for 3–4 minutes until golden, well sealed and nearly cooked through. Remove from the wok and set aside.

Add the peppers to the wok and stir-fry briskly over high heat for 2 minutes. Return the chicken to the wok and add the black bean sauce. Cook for another minute, stirring occasionally.

Meanwhile, combine the soy sauce, chicken stock and cornflour in a bowl with 2 tablespoons of cold water. Stir until smooth, then pour into the wok. Simmer gently for about 2 minutes until the sauce has thickened and the chicken is cooked through. Remove from the heat and sprinkle with the almonds, if using. Serve immediately with rice.

skinless chicken breasts 2 large, cut into 2cm (¾in) chunks

groundnut oil 1 tbsp

red pepper 1, deseeded and thinly sliced

yellow pepper 1, deseeded and thinly sliced

Chinese black bean sauce 2 tbsp

light soy sauce ½ tbsp

chicken stock 60ml (2fl oz)

cornflour 2 tsp

flaked almonds 1 tbsp

cooked microwave long grain rice 250g packet to serve, optional

for the marinade

Chinese rice wine or sherry ½ tbsp

light soy sauce 1 tbsp

sesame oil 1 tsp

caster sugar ½ tsp

grated fresh ginger 1 tsp

dried chilli flakes a pinch

QR Code
Scan with a smartphone for an ingredients shopping list.

68

*A colourful Chinese chicken dish that's
simple enough to create in no time.*

Cheaper and tastier than a take-away,
this dish is perfect for informal entertaining.

Gingered Chicken & Cashew Noodles

Time required 15 mins. Per portion: 580 Kcal, 31g fat (4.1g saturated)

Serves 4

Chinese rice wine or sherry 2 tbsp

cornflour 2 tsp

skinless chicken breasts 350g (12oz), cut into small chunks

dried egg noodles 175g (6oz)

groundnut or sunflower oil 3 tbsp

fresh ginger 3cm (1¼in), peeled and grated

mangetout 125g (4½oz), thinly sliced

snipped chives 4 tbsp

cashew nuts 125g (4½oz), toasted in a dry frying pan, then chopped

for the sauce

chicken stock 90ml (3fl oz)

dark soy sauce 2 tbsp

lemon juice 1 tbsp

sesame oil 1 tbsp

soft light brown sugar 2 tsp

QR Code
Scan with a smartphone for an ingredients shopping list.

Put the rice wine or sherry and cornflour into a bowl and mix well. Add the chicken, stir well and set aside to marinate while you prepare the remaining ingredients.

Prepare the noodles according to the packet's instructions, then drain and shake dry.

Put all the sauce ingredients into a small bowl and mix well.

Heat half the oil in a wok or large frying pan over a medium heat, then add the chicken and stir-fry for 5-8 minutes until golden. Remove to a plate and wipe the wok clean with kitchen paper.

Add the remaining oil, then the ginger and mangetout, and fry for 1 minute. Return the chicken to the wok, then add the noodles and sauce. Heat through for 2 minutes. Add the chives and cashew nuts, stir well and serve.

Moroccan Honey & Lemon Chicken

Time required 20 mins. Per portion: 214 Kcal, 4g fat (0.7g saturated)

Serves 4

Lightly season the chicken breasts with salt and pepper, then heat 1 tablespoon of the honey in a frying pan over a medium heat. Add the chicken and the garlic and gently fry the chicken breasts for 1 minute on each side until caramelised, but watch carefully to ensure that the honey doesn't burn.

Stir the tomatoes into the pan and add the remaining honey together with the cinnamon and lemon zest and juice. Bring to a simmer and cook, uncovered, for 15 minutes.

If using, make couscous or bulgar wheat according to the packet's instructions. Scatter the almonds over the chicken and serve.

skinless chicken breasts 4, about 125g (4½oz) each

salt and freshly ground black pepper

runny honey 3 tbsp

garlic 2 cloves, peeled and sliced

chopped tomatoes 400g can

ground cinnamon ½ tsp

lemon ½, grated rind and juice

couscous or bulgar wheat 2 x 60g packets, made according to packet's instructions, to serve, optional

flaked almonds 20g (¾oz)

QR Code
Scan with a smartphone for an ingredients shopping list.

72

Moroccan cuisine marries sweet and savoury flavours in this homely dish.

Thai-Flavour Pork

Time required 30 mins. Per portion: 320 Kcal, 20g fat (8.9g saturated)

Serves 4

desiccated coconut 4–5 tbsp

pork fillet 500g (1lb 2oz)

salt and freshly ground black pepper

vegetable or groundnut oil 3 tbsp

grated fresh ginger 1 tsp

garlic 3 cloves, peeled and thinly sliced

birdseye chillies 4, deseeded and chopped

lemongrass 1 stalk, halved and thinly sliced

Thai sweet chilli sauce 2 tbsp

Thai fish sauce 1 tbsp

basil a large handful

cooked microwave basmati and Thai rice 2 x 250g packets to serve, optional

QR Code
Scan with a smartphone for an ingredients shopping list.

Heat a wok or large frying pan over a medium heat and add the coconut when hot. Dry-fry for a few minutes until golden. Remove from the wok and set aside.

Place the pork fillet in between two large sheets of cling film, then bash with a rolling pin until about 2cm (¾in) thick. Slice very thinly and then season the pork with salt and pepper.

Heat 2 tbsp of the oil in the wok over a medium heat, then brown the pork in two or three batches, adding more oil if necessary. Remove and set aside.

Add the remaining oil, ginger, garlic, chillies and lemongrass to the wok and stir-fry for 1 minute. Return the pork to the wok and stir-fry for another 1 minute.

Add the chilli and fish sauces, and stir well. Cook for a further 2 minutes, or until the pork is completely cooked through. Stir in the basil. Remove from the heat and serve immediately on a bed of rice with the coconut sprinkled on the top.

Bacon & Eggs in a Pan

Time required 15 mins. Per portion: 400 Kcal, 30g fat (9g saturated)

Serves 3

Heat the oil in a large frying pan over a medium heat. Add the bacon and cook for 2 minutes until the bacon starts to brown and go crisp around the edges.

Break the eggs into a bowl, add salt and pepper and whisk lightly. Pour into the pan around the bacon, making sure the base is covered and the bacon sits half-submerged. Dot with the tomatoes and cook over a medium-low heat until the eggs have set. Sprinkle with chives and serve immediately, cut into wedges with hot buttered toast.

sunflower oil 1 tbsp

dry-cured back bacon 8 rashers

eggs 6 large

salt and freshly ground black pepper

cherry tomatoes 10, halved

finely snipped chives 2 tbsp

hot buttered toast to serve, optional

QR Code
Scan with a smartphone for an ingredients shopping list.

76

Pea & Bacon Risotto

Time required 30 mins. Per portion: 541 Kcal, 21g fat (8.1g saturated)

Serves 4

olive oil 2 tbsp

onion 1, peeled and chopped

rindless back bacon 175g (6oz), cut into thin strips

garlic 2 cloves, peeled and finely chopped

risotto rice 300g (11oz)

white wine 125ml (4fl oz)

hot chicken or vegetable stock about 900ml (1½ pints)

frozen peas 125g (4½oz)

full fat soft cheese 1–2 tbsp

freshly ground black pepper

Parmesan cheese shavings to serve

QR Code
Scan with a smartphone for an ingredients shopping list.

Heat the olive oil in a heavy-based saucepan over a medium heat. Add the onion, bacon and garlic and cook for about 5 minutes, stirring often. Add the rice to the pan and mix well in the cooking juices. Add the wine and simmer, stirring, until all the wine has been absorbed.

Begin adding the hot stock, a large ladle at a time, stirring until each ladleful has been absorbed by the rice. Continue until the rice is tender and creamy, but the grains still firm. (This should take 15–20 minutes depending on the type of rice used.) Stir in the frozen peas 5 minutes before the end of cooking.

When the rice is cooked, stir in the soft cheese and spoon into warmed bowls. Season with black pepper and serve with the Parmesan cheese.

Pepper & Chorizo Tortilla

Time required 30 mins. Per portion: 395 Kcal, 30g fat (10.5g saturated)

Serves 4

Heat the oil in a large lidded frying pan over a medium heat. Add the peppers and onion and cook for 3–5 minutes until golden brown. Add the garlic and chorizo and cook for 2–3 minutes.

Meanwhile, whisk the eggs in a bowl. Stir in the parsley, season with pepper to taste, then pour over the peppers in the pan. Sprinkle with the cheese.

Cover with a lid, reduce the heat to low and cook the tortilla for 10–12 minutes until it has set around the edges but is still barely wobbly in the middle. Loosen the sides and underneath with a plastic spatula. You should be able to slide the tortilla out of the pan and onto a plate, then flip onto another plate to serve bottom-side up. If it cannot be shaken out of the pan, put a large plate upside down over the frying pan, hold the edges with oven gloves and flip over to release the tortilla. Serve hot or cold with a large mixed salad.

- **olive oil** 2 tbsp
- **red pepper** 1, deseeded and thinly sliced
- **yellow pepper** 1, deseeded and thinly sliced
- **onion** 1, peeled and thinly sliced
- **garlic** 2 cloves, peeled and chopped
- **chorizo** 125g (4½oz), sliced
- **eggs** 6 large
- **chopped flat-leaf parsley** a handful
- **freshly ground black pepper**
- **Manchego cheese** 40g (1½oz), grated
- **mixed salad** to serve, optional

QR Code
Scan with a smartphone for an ingredients shopping list.

This rich, traditional Provençal dish is colourful and easy to make. It's so tasty you can serve simply with rustic bread.

Ratatouille

Time required 50 mins. Per portion: 155 Kcal, 8g fat (1.1g saturated)

Serves 6

olive oil 3 tbsp

onions 2 large, peeled and thinly sliced

garlic 2 cloves, peeled and crushed

finely crushed coriander seeds 2 tsp

white wine 5 tbsp

red, yellow or orange peppers 3, deseeded and sliced

aubergines 2, cubed

chopped tomatoes 400g can

caster sugar 1 tsp

black olives about 20

salt and freshly ground black pepper

basil leaves to garnish, optional

Heat the oil in a flameproof casserole or saucepan over a medium heat. Add the onions, garlic and coriander seeds and cook for about 4 minutes until soft and transparent, but not coloured. Add the wine and cook until the liquid has been absorbed.

Add the peppers and aubergines to the casserole and cook for about 10 minutes, stirring occasionally until softening around the edges, but not browning. Add the tomatoes, sugar and olives. Heat to simmering point, season well with salt and pepper, then half-cover and cook for about 25 minutes until the ratatouille is thick and the liquid has been absorbed. Garnish with basil, if using, and serve hot or cold.

83

QR Code
Scan with a smartphone for an ingredients shopping list.

Aubergine, Tomato & Lentil Curry

Time required 45 mins. Per portion: 221 Kcal, 10g fat (1.2g saturated)

Serves 4

Heat the oil in a lidded frying pan or saucepan set over a high heat until the oil is smoking hot. Add the aubergine and cook for 5 minutes, turning the pieces often so that they cook evenly. At first the aubergine will absorb the oil, but as it cooks to a dark and golden colour, the oil will start to seep out back into the pan. Remove the aubergine from the pan at this point and not before. Set aside.

Add the onion, garlic and ginger to the pan and cook for 5 minutes. Then add the cherry tomatoes and cook for 1 minute, until they just soften and collapse. Remove them from the pan before they break up too much. Set aside with the aubergine.

Add the curry leaves and cumin to the pan and cook for a couple of minutes while the curry leaves pop and crackle. Add the chilli powder, tomato purée, 450ml (16fl oz) of water and the lentils. Simmer for 15–20 minutes, until the lentils are tender but retain some 'bite'. Stir in the aubergine and tomatoes and cook the curry for a couple of minutes just to warm through. Season to taste and then stir in the coriander. Serve with naan bread.

olive oil 3 tbsp

aubergine 1 large, cubed

red onion 1, peeled and chopped

garlic 2 cloves, peeled and chopped

grated fresh ginger 1 tbsp

cherry tomatoes on the vine 250g (9oz)

curry leaves 6–8

ground cumin 1 tsp

chilli powder ¼ tsp

tomato purée 1 tbsp

red lentils 125g (4½oz)

salt and freshly ground black pepper

coriander a handful, chopped

warm naan bread to serve, optional

QR Code
Scan with a smartphone for an ingredients shopping list.

84

*A hearty and mildly spiced dish with a
beautiful orange hue, perfect for serving
with poppadoms and mango chutney.*

Rustic Vegetable Pilaf

Time required 1 hr. Per portion: 450 Kcal, 14g fat (1.4g saturated)

Serves 4

olive oil 2 tbsp

onion 1, peeled and chopped

garlic 2 cloves, peeled and chopped

grated fresh ginger 1 tbsp

red chilli 1 large, finely chopped

ground coriander 1 tsp

ground cumin 1 tsp

turmeric 1 tsp

flaked almonds 50g (2oz)

basmati rice 300g (11oz)

carrot 1, peeled and cut into chunks

pumpkin or squash 200g (7oz), peeled, deseeded and cut into chunks

sweet potato 1 small, peeled and cut into chunks

lime 1, juice only

salt and freshly ground black pepper

chopped coriander a handful

poppadoms and **mango chutney** to serve, optional

Heat the oil in a heavy-based saucepan over a high heat. Add the onion, garlic, ginger and chilli and cook for 5 minutes, stirring often.

Add the spices and almonds and cook for a further 5 minutes, until the spices become aromatic and look very dark in the pan.

Add the rice and cook for a minute, stirring well to coat the rice in the spices. Then add the carrot, pumpkin or squash and sweet potato to the pan.

Pour in 600ml (1 pint) of water and stir, loosening any grains of rice that are stuck to the bottom of the pan. Bring to the boil, cover with a lid, then reduce the heat to low and cook for 25 minutes, stirring occasionally. Add the lime juice, seasoning and coriander and stir well to combine. Serve with poppadoms and mango chutney, if you like.

QR Code
Scan with a smartphone for an ingredients shopping list.

Wild Mushroom Risotto

Time required 50 mins. Per portion: 534 Kcal, 22g fat (13.3g saturated)

Serves 6

Melt half the butter in a large heavy-based saucepan over a medium heat. Add the onion and garlic and cook for 10 minutes until soft, golden and translucent, but not browned. Stir in the mushrooms and herbs and then cook for 3 minutes.

Pour the wine or vermouth into the pan and boil until it has reduced and almost disappeared. Stir in the rice and fry with the onion and mushrooms for 1-2 minutes until dry and slightly opaque.

Begin adding the hot stock, a ladleful at a time, stirring until each ladleful has been absorbed by the rice. Continue until the rice is tender and creamy, but the grains still firm. (This should take 15–20 minutes depending on the type of rice used.)

Taste and season with salt and pepper. Stir in the remaining butter and the Parmesan cheese (or a vegetarian version), cover and leave to rest for a couple of minutes. Serve immediately with extra grated cheese.

unsalted butter 125g (4½oz)

onion 1 large, peeled and finely chopped

garlic 2 cloves, peeled and finely chopped

mixed wild mushrooms 250g (9oz), wiped and coarsely chopped

chopped thyme 1 tbsp

chopped marjoram 1 tbsp

dry white wine or vermouth 150ml (¼ pint)

risotto rice 500g (1lb 2oz)

hot vegetable stock about 1.5 litres (2½ pints)

salt and freshly ground black pepper

Parmesan-style hard cheese 75g (3oz), plus extra to serve, grated

QR Code
Scan with a smartphone for an ingredients shopping list.

Potato & Mushroom Gratin

Time required 1½ hrs. Per portion: 317 Kcal, 9g fat (1.9g saturated)

Serves 6

butter for greasing

potatoes 1kg (2 ¼ lb), peeled and thickly sliced

olive oil for sprinkling

flavoursome mushrooms such as dark flat cap, chestnut or portobello 750g (1lb 10oz), wiped, and thickly sliced

stale white breadcrumbs 175g (6oz)

grated Parmesan-style hard cheese 4 tbsp

chopped flat-leaf parsley 4 tbsp

salt and freshly ground black pepper

sliced beef tomatoes and cold meat to serve (if not serving vegetarians), optional

Preheat the oven to 180°C/350°F/Gas 4 and thoroughly butter a large ovenproof dish.

Put half the potatoes in a layer in the bottom of the dish, sprinkle with oil and cover with half the mushrooms.

Put the breadcrumbs, Parmesan cheese (or vegetarian version), parsley and salt and pepper in a bowl and mix well. Spread half this mixture over the mushrooms, then sprinkle with more oil. Cover with a second layer of potatoes, then a layer of the remaining mushrooms. Finally, sprinkle with the rest of the breadcrumb mixture and more oil.

Cover with foil and bake for 30 minutes. Uncover and cook for a further 30 minutes until the potatoes are tender and the top is golden brown. Serve immediately with sliced tomatoes and cold meat (if using).

91

QR Code
Scan with a smartphone for an ingredients shopping list.

Jacket Potatoes with Tuna & Tarragon Mayonnaise

Time required 1½ hrs. Per portion: 365 Kcal, 11g fat (1.8g saturated)

Serves 2

Preheat the oven to 200°C/400°F/Gas 6. Put the potatoes in a small roasting tin, prick several times with a fork, drizzle each with a teaspoon of oil and turn so they are coated all over. Sprinkle with a little salt, to help make the potato skin go crisp, and bake for 1–1¼ hours or until the potatoes are tender.

Mix the tuna with the tarragon and enough mayonnaise to bind. Season with the lime juice and salt and pepper to taste.

When the potatoes are ready, split in half. Divide the tuna mix between the potatoes and serve with a mixed salad and a sprinkling of black pepper, if wished.

baking potatoes 2, about 250g (9oz) each

olive oil 2 tsp

salt and freshly ground black pepper

tuna chunks in brine 185g can, drained

chopped tarragon 2 tbsp

light mayonnaise 3–4 tbsp

lime ½–1, juice only

mixed salad leaves to serve, optional

QR Code
Scan with a smartphone for an ingredients shopping list.

This dish is full of flavour and perfect for a cosy dinner by the fire. Enjoy with a simple cucumber salad and warmed chapatis.

Chicken & Lentil Curry

Time required 45 mins. Per portion: 388 Kcal, 9g fat (4.4g saturated)

Serves 4

unsalted butter 25g (1oz)

onions 2 large, peeled and thinly sliced

garlic 2 cloves, peeled and crushed

garam masala 1½ tbsp

passata 300g (11oz)

bay or curry leaves 8

red lentils 110g (4oz)

chicken stock 400ml (14fl oz)

skinless chicken breasts 4, about 500g (1lb 2oz), cubed

salt and freshly ground black pepper

coriander leaves to garnish, optional

warm chapatis or naan bread to serve, optional

for the cucumber yogurt

plain yogurt 140ml pot

cucumber ¼, cut into ribbons or chopped

QR Code
Scan with a smartphone for an ingredients shopping list.

Melt the butter in a lidded deep frying pan or a saucepan over a medium heat. Add the onions and fry, stirring, until they are sizzling. Cover with a lid, reduce the heat and cook for 10–15 minutes, stirring occasionally, until the onions have softened.

Add the garlic and garam masala and cook for a further 3–4 minutes until the spices start to release their aroma and the onions are beginning to turn golden. Add the passata, bay or curry leaves, lentils, stock and chicken. Cover with a lid and simmer for 15-25 minutes until the lentils are tender (adding more stock if necessary).

To make the cucumber yogurt, put the yogurt in a small dish, add a good pinch of salt and stir in the cucumber.

When the curry is cooked, remove the bay or curry leaves and season generously with salt and pepper (lentils tend to absorb a lot of seasoning). Transfer to bowls, scatter with coriander, if using, serve with cucumber yogurt and warm chapatis or naan bread.

95

Spicy Chicken Tagine

Time required 50 mins. Per portion: 824 Kcal, 55g fat (15.9g saturated)

Serves 4

Heat the oil and butter in a tagine or flameproof casserole over a medium heat. Add the onion, chopped rosemary, ginger and chillies and cook for about 4 minutes until the onion begins to soften.

Add the chicken thighs and brown them on both sides. Stir in the halved rosemary sprigs and the cinnamon sticks. Add the apricots with the honey, then stir in the tomatoes with their juice. (Add a little water, if necessary, to ensure there is enough liquid to cover the base of the tagine and submerge the apricots.) Bring the liquid to the boil, then reduce the heat. Cover with a lid and cook gently for 35–40 minutes until the chicken is cooked through.

Remove the cinnamon sticks and rosemary sprigs and then season with salt and pepper to taste. Sprinkle the basil over the chicken and serve the dish immediately with couscous.

olive oil 2 tbsp

unsalted butter 15g (½oz)

onion 1, peeled and finely chopped

rosemary 3 sprigs, 1 finely chopped, the other 2 cut in half

fresh ginger 40g (1½oz), peeled and grated

red chillies 1-2, deseeded and finely chopped

skinless boneless chicken thighs 8

cinnamon sticks 1–2

dried apricots 175g (6oz)

runny honey 2 tbsp

plum tomatoes 400g can

salt and freshly ground black pepper

fresh basil leaves a small bunch, the larger leaves shredded

couscous 200g (7oz), made according to the packet's instructions, to serve, optional

QR Code
Scan with a smartphone for an ingredients shopping list.

Wholesome and traditional, yet simple to prepare, this chicken and barley recipe is the perfect meal-in-a-dish.

Chicken & Barley Supper

Time required 2 hrs. Per portion: 350 Kcal, 4g fat (1.3g saturated)

Serves 4

wholemeal flour 2 tbsp

freshly ground black pepper

skinless chicken breasts 4, about 500g (1lb 2oz), cubed

lean bacon rashers 4, about110g (4oz), cut into strips

onions 2, peeled and chopped

carrots 2, peeled and sliced

celery sticks 2, chopped

white wine or chicken stock 750–900ml (1¼–1½ pints)

pearl barley 3 tbsp, rinsed

mixed chopped herbs, such as **parsley, rosemary, basil and thyme** 1 tbsp

chopped flat-leaf parsley to serve

microwave vegetables to serve, optional

QR Code
Scan with a smartphone for an ingredients shopping list.

Put the flour in a bowl and season with pepper, then toss the chicken in the flour. Heat a large lidded frying pan or saucepan over a medium heat, add the bacon and dry-fry for 5 minutes, stirring frequently, until the fat starts to run. Then add the chicken and fry gently for 5–8 minutes, turning frequently, until the chicken is sealed all over. Remove the chicken and bacon from the pan with a slotted spoon and set aside.

Add the onions, carrots, celery and 4 tablespoons of the wine or stock to the pan and gently fry for about 5 minutes until the vegetables are softened. Add the pearl barley, herbs and 600ml (1 pint) of the wine or stock. Cover with a lid and bring to the boil, then reduce the heat and simmer for 1 hour. Add more wine or stock as it is absorbed.

Return the chicken and bacon to the pan and continue to simmer for a further 30 minutes, or until the pearl barley and chicken are tender. Stir occasionally during cooking, adding a little more wine or stock, if necessary. Serve, sprinkled with chopped parsley and accompanied by a selection of your favourite vegetables.

Lemony Chicken with Leeks

Time required 1 hr. Per portion: 695 Kcal, 45g fat (11.8g saturated)

Serves 4

Put the flour in a bowl and season with salt and pepper, then toss the chicken in the flour.

Heat the oil in a large frying pan over a medium heat. Add the leeks and stir-fry for about 4 minutes until softened and silky. Remove the leeks and set aside. Add half of the chicken to the pan and cook for 4–5 minutes, turning each piece often, until golden brown all over. Transfer the browned chicken to a plate and repeat to cook the remaining chicken.

Pour off all but 1 tablespoon of oil from the pan, leaving any sediment in the pan. Add the garlic and lemon slices and cook for 1 minute, stirring well. Add the wine and leave to sizzle for 1 minute, then add the lemon juice, chicken stock and soy sauce and bring to the boil.

Return the chicken to the pan and cook for 20 minutes. Turn each piece of chicken, then put the leeks on top of the chicken. Cover the pan with foil and cook for a further 20 minutes, until the chicken is cooked through. Stir to combine the chicken and any of the cooking juices evenly with the leeks. Serve with couscous mixed with pine nuts.

plain flour 60g (2½oz)

salt and freshly ground black pepper

whole chicken 1, about 1.6kg (3½lb), cut into 10 pieces

olive oil 125ml (4fl oz)

baby leeks 12

garlic 3 cloves, peeled and chopped

lemon 1, thickly sliced

white wine 125ml (4fl oz)

lemon juice 125ml (4fl oz)

chicken stock 125ml (4fl oz)

light soy sauce 1 tbsp

couscous 200g (7oz), made according to the packet's instructions, to serve, optional

pine nuts to serve, optional

QR Code
Scan with a smartphone for an ingredients shopping list.

Coq au Vin

Time required 1½ hrs. Per portion: 594 Kcal, 41g fat (13.3g saturated)

Serves 6

olive oil 3 tbsp

shallots 8, peeled and halved

unsmoked rindless streaky bacon
225g (8oz), cut into strips

garlic 2 cloves, peeled and finely
chopped

closed cup white mushrooms 225g
(8oz), wiped and halved

chicken thighs 6

chicken breast fillets 3, cut in half

red wine 1 bottle

dried thyme a large pinch

butter 25g (1oz), softened

plain flour 25g (1oz)

**salt and freshly ground black
pepper**

chopped flat-leaf parsley 2 tbsp,
optional

ready-made mashed potato 3 x
450g pots to serve , optional

green leaf salad with vinaigrette to
serve, optional

QR Code
Scan with a
smartphone
for an ingredients
shopping list.

Heat the oil in a large flameproof casserole or
saucepan over a medium heat. Add the shallots
and cook for about 5 minutes until golden. Remove
from the casserole and set aside. Add the bacon,
garlic and mushrooms and cook for 7–10 minutes,
stirring frequently. Remove from the casserole
using a slotted spoon and set aside.

Add the chicken, making sure it fits in a single
layer at the bottom, and cook in the hot oil for
10–15 minutes until browned, turning frequently
(you may need to do this in two batches). Return
the bacon and vegetables to the pot, pour in the
red wine, then stir in the dried thyme, cover with
a lid and bring to the boil. Reduce the heat and
simmer for 30–40 minutes, stirring occasionally.

Meanwhile, beat together the butter and flour in
a bowl to make a smooth paste. When the chicken
is cooked, gradually add small spoonfuls of the
paste to the simmering casserole, stirring well
after each addition. Cook for a further 5 minutes
until you have a smooth, thick and glossy red wine
sauce. If the skin has come off the meat, remove it
from the casserole.

Season with salt and pepper to taste and serve,
garnished with the parsley, with mash and salad
dressed with a little vinaigrette.

103

Chicken with Chorizo & Potatoes

Time required 1½ hrs. Per portion: 1086 Kcal, 76g fat (23.9g saturated)

Serves 4

Preheat the oven to 190°C/375°F/Gas 5. Heat the oil in a large flameproof casserole over a medium heat. Add the chorizo, onion and garlic and cook for about 5 minutes until the onion is softened. Add the chicken, making sure it fits in a single layer at the bottom of the casserole, increase the heat if necessary and cook for about 10 minutes until the chicken is beginning to brown, stirring often.

Add the potatoes and cook for a further 5 minutes, stirring continuously. Add the remaining ingredients, then half-fill the empty can of tomatoes with water and add to the casserole. Mix well, cover with a lid and bring to the boil.

Transfer the casserole to the oven and cook for 40–45 minutes until the chicken and potatoes are cooked through. After 20 minutes, remove from the oven and mix well, adding a little more boiling water if the mixture is becoming too dry. Serve in warmed bowls with crusty bread.

olive oil 2 tbsp

cooking chorizo sausage 225g packet, sliced

large onion 1, peeled and finely chopped

garlic 2 cloves, peeled and finely chopped

chicken thighs 8

potatoes 600g (1lb 6oz), scrubbed and diced

chopped tomatoes 400g can

chicken stock cube 1, crumbled

dried mixed herbs 1 tsp

salt and freshly ground black pepper

crusty bread to serve, optional

QR Code
Scan with a smartphone for an ingredients shopping list.

104

Oven-Roasted Spicy Macaroni

Time required 1 hr. Per portion: 656 Kcal, 27g fat (9.7g saturated)

Serves 4

cherry tomatoes 250g (9oz)

red onion 1, peeled and finely chopped

garlic 2 cloves, peeled and finely chopped

olive oil 2 tbsp

small macaroni 300g (11oz)

skinless and boneless chicken thighs 4, quartered

chorizo 200g (7oz), thickly sliced

chopped rosemary 2 tsp

chicken stock 1 litre (1¾ pints)

saffron threads a pinch

salt and freshly ground black pepper

large uncooked prawns 8, thawed if frozen

torn basil a handful, to serve

QR Code
Scan with a smartphone for an ingredients shopping list.

Preheat the oven to 220°C/425°F/Gas 7.

Put the cherry tomatoes into a roasting tin and sprinkle with the onion, garlic and oil. Roast in the oven for 20 minutes until the tomatoes are soft.

Remove the tin from the oven and add the macaroni, chicken, chorizo, rosemary, stock and saffron and season with salt and pepper. Mix well and return it to the oven to bake for 30 minutes.

Stir in the prawns and bake for a further 5 minutes until the pasta, prawns and chicken are cooked. Sprinkle with basil and serve.

107

Chicken, Sausage & Rice

Time required 1½ hrs. Per portion: 824 Kcals, 43g fat (13.5g saturated)

Serves 4–6

Preheat the oven to 200°C/400°F/Gas 6. Bundle the bay leaf, thyme and parsley with kitchen string.

Heat the oil in a large flameproof casserole over a high heat. Add the chicken pieces, skin-side down, and cook for 3–5 minutes until browned. Repeat on the other side (you may need to do this in batches.) Transfer the browned chicken to a plate and season with salt and pepper.

Add the sausages to the pan and cook for about 10 minutes until browned. Remove and cut into 3–4 pieces, depending on their size, and set aside.

Add the onion, red pepper and celery and cook on high heat for 2–3 minutes until they begin to brown. Add the garlic, chilli flakes and salt and pepper and cook for 1 minute more.

Stir in the rice until all the grains are coated, then add the wine, stock and tomatoes and mix well. Add the herbs, the chicken and sausage.

Cover and bake in the oven for about 30 minutes until the rice is cooked. After 20 minutes, add the peas and a little water if the liquid has almost completely evaporated. Cook for 10 minutes more. Remove from the oven and set aside, still covered, for 10 minutes. Remove the bunch of herbs and fluff up the rice to mix in the peas. Serve with a green salad.

bay leaf 1

thyme a few sprigs

flat-leaf parsley a few sprigs

olive oil 1 tbsp

chicken thighs 8

salt and freshly ground black pepper

pork sausages 6

onion 1, peeled and chopped

red pepper 1, deseeded and chopped

celery sticks 2, chopped

garlic 3 cloves, peeled and finely chopped

dried chilli flakes ¼–½ tsp

paella rice 375g (13oz), or other short-grained rice

red or white dry wine 125ml (4fl oz)

chicken stock 300ml (½ pint)

chopped tomatoes 400g can

peas 200g (7oz)

green salad to serve, optional

QR Code
Scan with a smartphone for an ingredients shopping list.

Pork & Bean Casserole

Time required 2 hrs. Per portion: 839 Kcal, 46g fat (15.1g saturated)

Serves 6

olive oil 4 tbsp

carrots 350g (12oz), peeled and cut into 3cm (1¼in) chunks

onions 4, peeled but left whole

turnips 4 small, scrubbed

thyme 1 sprig

bay leaf 1

peppercorns 6

garlic 6 cloves, peeled and chopped

hand of pork 2kg (4½lb)

smoked bacon lardons 200-250g pack

canned cannellini beans 400g (14oz), drained and rinsed

salt and freshly ground black pepper

small potatoes 750g (1lb 10oz), peeled

green beans 250g (9oz)

QR Code
Scan with a
smartphone
for an ingredients
shopping list.

Preheat the oven to 170°C/325°F/Gas 3.

Heat the oil in a large flameproof casserole over a medium heat. Stir in the carrots, onions, turnips, thyme, bay leaf, peppercorns and garlic and cook for about 4 minutes until softened but not browned.

Meanwhile, cut the rind off the pork and reserve it. Add the pork, its rind, the bacon lardons and cannellini beans to the casserole. Cover with water, add salt and pepper and bring to the boil on top of the stove. Transfer to the oven and simmer for about 1½ hours until the beans are tender.

After 1 hour, taste and adjust the seasoning, then add the potatoes for the last 30 minutes and the green beans for the last 5 minutes.

To serve, remove and discard the pork rind and the bay leaf. Carve the pork into thick slices. Serve with the vegetables and cooking juices.

111

Roast Belly of Pork with Hoisin Sauce

Time required 2 hrs. Per portion: 531 Kcal, 30g fat (10.7g saturated)

Serves 4

Preheat the oven to 230°C/450°F/Gas 8. Check the weight of the pork and calculate the cooking time: allow 45 minutes per 500g (1lb 2oz), plus 40 minutes. Lay the pork in a roasting tin, skin-side up. Mix together the oil and five spice stir-fry paste and smear on both sides of the meat. Turn it back so the joint is skin side-up and roast for 10 minutes. Then reduce the oven temperature to 190°C/375°F/Gas 5 and roast for half of the remaining cooking time.

Remove the pork from the oven and spread the hoisin sauce on both sides of the meat. Baste with the cooking juices and return to the oven for the remainder of the cooking time, basting with the sauce every 20 minutes.

Remove from the oven and leave to rest on a board for 10 minutes. Then remove the fat from the pork, slice the meat thinly and use it to fill baps or warmed tortillas. Top with the spring onions and cucumber.

boneless pork belly joint about 680g (1½lb), skin left on and scored

olive oil 2 tbsp

five spice stir-fry paste 1 tsp

hoisin sauce 2 tbsp

baps or tortillas 4

spring onions 4–6, trimmed and finely sliced

cucumber ½, finely shredded

QR Code
Scan with a smartphone for an ingredients shopping list.

114

Spices work wonderfully with red cabbage and perfectly
complement the pork in this dish. Serve with mash and
gravy for a delicious Sunday lunch.

Roast Pork with
Red Cabbage & Cider

Time required 2 hrs. Per portion: 523 Kcal, 28g fat (10.8g saturated)

Serves 6

boneless crackling pork loin joint about 1.1kg (2½lb)

salt and freshly ground black pepper

red cabbage 500g (1lb 2oz), quartered, cored and finely shredded

pink lady apple 1, quartered, cored and finely chopped

ground mixed spice a generous pinch

strong cider 568ml bottle

ready-made mashed potato 2-3 x 450g pots to serve, optional

instant gravy to serve, optional

QR Code
Scan with a smartphone for an ingredients shopping list.

Preheat the oven to 220°C/425°F/Gas 7. Check the weight of the pork and calculate the cooking time: allow 25 minutes per 500g (1lb 2oz), plus 25 minutes. Sit the pork in a roasting tin, skin-side up. Liberally season it with salt and pepper and arrange the red cabbage and apple around it. Season the red cabbage mix and add the mixed spice and 300ml (½ pint) of the cider, making sure it does not go over the crackling.

Roast the pork in the preheated oven for 30 minutes. Remove from the oven, stir the red cabbage mix, add the rest of the cider, and stir again. Then reduce the oven temperature to 180°C/350°F/Gas 4 and roast for 30 minutes. Stir the red cabbage once or twice during cooking.

To make sure the crackling is crisp, increase the oven temperature back up to 220°C/425°F/Gas 7. Remove the pork from the oven and cover the cabbage with strips of foil to prevent it from scorching, then return the tin back to the oven and leave until the end of the calculated cooking time.

Remove the pork from the roasting tin and leave it to stand for 10–15 minutes before carving. Cover the red cabbage with foil and keep warm. Serve the mash and red cabbage with slices of pork and a ladleful of instant gravy.

Lamb & Broad Bean Tagine

Time required 2 hrs. Per portion: 554 Kcal, 35g fat (16g saturated)

Serves 6

Put the lamb in a large bowl and toss with the cinnamon, cumin, chilli powder, turmeric, saffron and white pepper. Heat 1 tablespoon of the oil in a tagine or heavy-based saucepan over a high heat, then add half the lamb. Cook for a few minutes, stirring occasionally, until the lamb is evenly browned, then tip it into a bowl. Add the rest of the oil to the tagine dish and brown the remainder of the lamb.

Put all the lamb back into the tagine with the onions, garlic, stock and a large pinch of salt. Cover with a lid and bring the mixture to the boil, then reduce the heat and simmer gently for 1 hour.

Add the dates to the tagine and simmer for a further 20 minutes. Then add the broad beans and simmer for a further 10 minutes. The meat should be so tender that it falls apart easily. Garnish with coriander and serve with couscous.

boneless shoulder of lamb or shoulder chops 1kg (2lb 4oz), cut into large chunks

ground cinnamon 2 tsp

ground cumin 2 tsp

hot chilli powder ½ tsp

ground turmeric 1 tsp

saffron threads a pinch

ground white pepper ½ tsp

olive oil 2 tbsp

onions 3, peeled and chopped

garlic 3 cloves, peeled and crushed

hot lamb stock 600ml (1 pint)

salt

pitted dates 150g (5oz)

podded broad beans 200g (7oz) fresh or frozen

coriander to garnish

couscous 200g (7oz), made according to the packet's instructions, to serve, optional

QR Code
Scan with a smartphone for an ingredients shopping list.

Lamb Navarin

Time required 2 hrs. Per portion: 518 Kcal, 26g fat (9.9g saturated)

Serves 4

olive oil 2 tbsp

boneless leg or shoulder of lamb
750g (1lb 10oz), excess fat removed
and the meat cubed

plain flour 2 tbsp

vegetable stock 450ml (¾ pint)

chopped tomatoes 400g can

tomato purée 1 tbsp

red wine 150ml (¼ pint)

bay leaves 2

marjoram 2 sprigs

smoked paprika ½ tsp

garlic 2 cloves, peeled and crushed

shallots 8, finely chopped

salt and freshly ground black pepper

baby carrots 300g (11oz)

new potatoes 300g (11oz), scrubbed
and larger ones halved

celery sticks 3, cut into chunks

runner beans 110g (4oz), chopped

curly kale or other greens 50g (2oz),
coarsely chopped

garlic bread to serve, optional

Heat the oil in a large flameproof casserole or saucepan over a medium heat. Add the lamb and cook briefly until it is browned all over. You may have to do this in batches.

Return all the meat to the pan, sprinkle with a fine dusting of flour, mix well and repeat until all the flour has been incorporated. Add the stock, chopped tomatoes, tomato purée, wine, herbs, paprika, garlic and shallots.

Cover and bring to the boil. Then reduce the heat and simmer for 1 hour, stirring from time to time. Add salt and pepper to taste.

Add the carrots, potatoes and celery and cook for 15 minutes. Then add the runner beans and curly kale or greens and stir gently. Cover and cook for a further 5 minutes or until the vegetables are cooked through. Remove the bay leaves and serve with garlic bread.

QR Code
Scan with a
smartphone
for an ingredients
shopping list.

Spring Lamb Stew

Time required **2 hrs.** *Per portion: 802 Kcal, 57g fat (27.4g saturated)*

Serves 4

Heat the oil in a large flameproof casserole or saucepan over a medium heat. Add the lamb and cook briefly until it is browned all over. You may have to do this in batches.

Return all the meat to the pan, reduce the heat slightly and stir in a pinch of salt and the flour. Cook, stirring to coat evenly, for 1 minute. Add the tomatoes and garlic. Stir in the stock, bay leaf and thyme, then bring to the boil and skim off any foam that rises to the surface. Reduce the heat, then cover and simmer for 50 minutes.

Add the carrots, leeks and turnips and cook for a further 25 minutes. Taste and adjust the seasoning with salt and pepper. Then add the peas and cook for about 7 minutes until the vegetables are cooked through and the meat is tender. Remove the bay leaf, sprinkle with the parsley and serve immediately with mash if you like.

sunflower oil 1 tbsp

lamb neck fillet 680g (1½lb), cubed

lamb chump chops 500g (1lb 2oz), each one cut into several pieces

salt and freshly ground black pepper

plain flour 1 tbsp

chopped tomatoes ½ 400g can

garlic 2 cloves, peeled and crushed

lamb or chicken stock 600ml (1 pint)

bay leaf 1

thyme a sprig

baby carrots 4

baby leeks 200g (7oz)

turnips 200g (7oz), peeled and cut into 3cm (1¼in) pieces

sugar snap peas 200g (7oz)

flat-leaf parsley a handful, chopped, optional

ready-made mashed potato 2 x 450g pots to serve, optional

QR Code
Scan with a smartphone for an ingredients shopping list.

Main Courses: Take it Easy

A huge colourful stew based on a traditional Portuguese recipe, which is perfect for an informal family gathering.

Lamb Stew with Piri Piri

Time required 1¾ hrs plus marinating. Per portion: 528 Kcal, 26g fat (10.8g saturated)

Serves 6

boneless lamb 1kg (2lb 4oz), cubed

olive oil 2 tbsp

plain flour 1½ tbsp

potatoes 500g (1lb 2oz), peeled and cut into large chunks

carrots 500g (1lb 2oz), peeled and cut into large pieces

salt and freshly ground black pepper

piri piri sauce 1–2 tsp

courgettes 750g (1lb 10oz), cut into large pieces

red pepper 1, deseeded and cut into large pieces

chickpeas 400g can, drained and rinsed

lemon, mint and parsley couscous 2 x 100g packets to serve, optional

for the marinade

onion 1, peeled and chopped

sherry vinegar 6 tbsp

sweet smoked paprika 1½ tsp

garlic 4 cloves, peeled and sliced

coriander a large handful, chopped

parsley a large handful, chopped

salt 1 tbsp

To make the marinade, combine all the ingredients in a bowl and mix well. Add the lamb, combine well, cover and marinate in the refrigerator for at least 3 hours or overnight.

Preheat the oven to 190°C/375°F/Gas 5.

Heat the oil in a large flameproof casserole over a medium heat. Add the lamb and all the marinade. Sprinkle with the flour and stir to coat well. Cook for 3–5 minutes to sear the meat, then stir in 250ml (9fl oz) of water. Add the potatoes, carrots, salt and the piri piri sauce and mix well. Cover with a lid and bake in the oven for 50 minutes.

Add the courgettes and red pepper and continue cooking for another 40 minutes. Remove from the oven and stir in the chickpeas. Add salt and pepper to taste, and more piri piri if you like. Serve hot, with couscous, if using.

123

QR Code
Scan with a smartphone for an ingredients shopping list.

Slow-Cooked Lamb Shanks

Time required 3½ hrs. Per portion: 980 Kcal, 55g fat (25g saturated)

Serves 4

Preheat the oven to 170°C/325°F/Gas 3. Season the flour and then gently roll the lamb shanks in it, reserving any flour that is left over.

Heat 2 tablespoons of the oil in a large flameproof casserole over a medium heat. Add the lamb and cook for about 10 minutes, turning often, until it is brown on all sides. Remove the lamb from the casserole with a slotted spoon and set aside.

Add the vegetables and the remaining oil and cook for about 5 minutes until they start to brown, stirring every so often. Add the reserved flour and stir in the redcurrant jelly. Gradually pour in the wine and stock and slowly bring the mixture to the boil, stirring constantly.

Return the lamb to the casserole and baste it in the hot liquid. Reduce the temperature and bring back to a simmer. Cover and bake in the oven for 1 hour. Then remove the casserole from the oven, turn the lamb and stir well. Cover once more and cook in the oven for a further 1½–2 hours until the meat and vegetables are tender. Stir the lamb a couple of times during cooking.

Season to taste and, if necessary, add more redcurrant jelly. Serve the lamb shanks on a bed of the vegetables with a spoonful of mashed potato.

salt and freshly ground black pepper

flour 2 tbsp

lamb shanks 4, about 1.6kg (3½lb) in total

olive oil 4 tbsp

onion 1 large, peeled and finely chopped

garlic 2 cloves, peeled and finely chopped

carrots 400g (14oz), peeled and cut into chunky batons

celery sticks 4, trimmed and cut into chunky slices

redcurrant jelly 2 tbsp

red wine 350ml (12fl oz)

lamb or chicken stock 350ml (12fl oz)

ready-made mashed potato 2 x 450g pots to serve, optional

QR Code
Scan with a smartphone for an ingredients shopping list.

Pot Roast Leg of Lamb with Rice & Tomatoes

Time required 2½ hrs. Per portion: 699 Kcal, 30g fat (11.3g saturated)

Serves 4

oil 3 tbsp

onion 1, peeled and chopped

garlic 2 cloves, peeled and finely chopped

aubergine 1, trimmed and diced

red pepper 1, deseeded and diced

half leg of lamb 1.1kg (2½lb), excess fat removed

passata 500g carton

rosemary 3 sprigs

risotto rice 200g (7oz)

salt and freshly ground black pepper

QR Code
Scan with a smartphone for an ingredients shopping list.

Preheat the oven to 170°C/325°F/Gas 3. Heat 2 tablespoons of the oil in a large flameproof casserole over a medium-low heat. Add the onion, garlic, aubergine and pepper and cook for 5–10 minutes, stirring frequently, until the vegetables start to soften. Remove the vegetables from the casserole with a slotted spoon and set aside.

Heat the remaining oil in the casserole. Add the lamb and cook for about 5 minutes, turning often, until it is brown on all sides. Return the vegetables to the pot, then add the passata. Fill the empty passata carton with water and add to the casserole. Mix well, set the rosemary sprigs on top of the lamb, cover and bring to the boil before transferring to the oven and baking for 1¼ hours.

Remove the casserole from the oven and stir the rice carefully into the liquid surrounding the lamb. Return the casserole to the oven without the lid and cook for 30 minutes. Then remove from the oven and check to see if the rice and lamb are cooked and the liquid has evaporated; if not, return the pot to the oven for a further 10-20 minutes and check again. If the liquid evaporates too quickly, add a splash of boiling water.

Remove the rosemary and season to taste. Cut the lamb into slices and serve on a bed of the risotto.

Chilli con Carne

Time required 1½ hrs. Per portion: 465 Kcal, 23g fat (8.8g saturated)

Serves 4-6

Heat the oil in a large saucepan over a medium-low heat. Add the garlic, onions, celery and carrot and cook gently for about 10 minutes until the vegetables are tender. Add the minced beef, breaking it up with a wooden spoon, and cook for a further 10 minutes until browned all over.

Add the oregano, bay leaves, tomato purée, passata, cayenne, paprika, wine and beans. Season with salt and pepper and mix well. Cover and simmer for 1 hour, stirring frequently.

Just before serving, remove the bay leaves and stir in the coriander. Serve with rice and guacamole.

olive oil 2 tbsp

garlic 3 cloves, peeled and crushed

onions 2, peeled and diced

celery stick 1, diced

carrot 1, peeled and diced

minced beef 680g (1½lb)

dried oregano 1 tsp

bay leaves 2

tomato purée 2 tbsp

passata 1 litre (1¾ pints)

cayenne pepper 1-2 tsp

paprika 1 tbsp

red wine 175ml (6fl oz)

red kidney beans 2 x 400g cans, drained and rinsed

salt and freshly ground black pepper

coriander a handful, chopped

cooked long grain microwave rice 2-3 x 250g packets to serve, optional

guacamole to serve, optional

QR Code
Scan with a smartphone for an ingredients shopping list.

128

This makes for a quirky meal – simple yet impressive, it should provide a talking point at the dinner table.

Baked Stuffed Pumpkin

Time required 1½ hrs. Per portion: 588 Kcal, 35g fat (12.1g saturated)

Serves 4

pumpkin or squash 1 large, about 3kg (6½lb)

olive oil 3 tbsp

smoked bacon 4 rashers, chopped

onions 1–2, peeled and thinly sliced

carrots 1–2, peeled and sliced

garlic 3 cloves, peeled and crushed

fresh ginger 3cm (1¼in), peeled and grated

oregano or thyme finely chopped leaves from 3–4 sprigs, chopped

minced beef 500g (1lb 2oz)

tomato purée 2 tsp

red chillies 1–2, halved, deseeded and chopped

cooked long grain microwave rice 250g packet

flat-leaf parsley leaves from 1 large bunch, chopped

salt and freshly ground black pepper

QR Code
Scan with a smartphone for an ingredients shopping list.

Preheat the oven to 200°C/400°F/Gas 6.

Using a small, sharp knife, cut the top off the pumpkin and reserve. Scoop out and discard all the seeds and fibres. Brush the inside of the pumpkin with 1 tablespoon of oil.

Heat the remaining oil in a large frying pan over a medium-high heat. Add the bacon and stir-fry for about 4 minutes until crispy. Remove with a slotted spoon and drain on kitchen paper.

Add the onions and carrots to the pan and cook for about 4 minutes until softened and translucent. Add the garlic and ginger and stir-fry for a further 2-3 minutes until the onion is golden. Add the oregano or thyme and the beef and stir-fry for about 5 minutes until the meat is browned all over. Stir in the tomato purée and chillies. Add the bacon and rice and stir-fry until hot.

Mix in the parsley, then use the mixture to stuff the pumpkin or squash – the mixture is already cooked, so it won't expand. Put the lid on top and envelop the bottom of the pumpkin in a 'basin' of foil. Bake in the oven for 45–60 minutes until the pumpkin is tender. Test with the point of a skewer – the time will depend on the pumpkin or squash variety and its size.

131

Meatballs in Tomato Sauce

Time required 50 mins. Per portion: 482 Kcal, 32g fat (13g saturated)

Serves 4

Mix together the beef, 1 garlic clove, breadcrumbs, egg, herbs and salt and pepper in a bowl. Divide the meatballs into 24 small balls, each the size of a large marble. Press a small cube of cheese into the centre of each and re-roll into a ball. Then put the meatballs onto a plate, cover with cling film and chill in the refrigerator while cooking the onions.

Heat 2 tablespoons of the oil in a large heavy-based frying pan over a medium heat. Add the onions and cook for about 5 minutes until they have softened. Add the remaining garlic and cook for about a minute and then add the meatballs with a tablespoon of extra oil, if necessary, and cook for 10 minutes, turning the meatballs twice.

Gently stir in the chopped tomatoes and bring slowly to the boil. Reduce the heat and simmer for 5–10 minutes until the meatballs are cooked through. If the sauce becomes too thick, add a splash of water. Remove the frying pan from the heat and season with salt and pepper to taste.

Serve the meatballs on a bed of rice with a generous spoonful of the tomato sauce and topped with the grated Cheddar cheese.

minced beef 500g (1lb 2oz)

garlic 3 cloves, peeled and finely chopped

fine breadcrumbs 2 tbsp

egg 1

dried mixed herbs 1 tsp

salt and freshly ground black pepper

Cheddar cheese 50g (2oz), cut into 24 small squares, plus extra grated cheese, to serve

olive oil 2–3 tbsp

onions 2, peeled and finely chopped

chopped tomatoes 2 x 400g cans

cooked microwave wholegrain rice 2 x 250g packets to serve, optional

QR Code
Scan with a smartphone for an ingredients shopping list.

Vietnamese-Style Beef

Time required 2¼ hrs plus marinating. *Per portion: 445 Kcal, 22g fat (7.8g saturated)*

Serves 4

boneless beef (shin or chuck) 1kg (2lb 4oz), cut into 3cm (1¼in) cubes

groundnut oil 2 tbsp

tomato purée 2 tbsp

tomatoes 3, skinned, deseeded and chopped

spring onions 6, shredded, to serve

sprigs of mint to serve, optional

for the marinade

lemongrass 1 stalk, peeled and finely chopped

mint 3 sprigs, leaves chopped

fish sauce 2 tbsp

light soft brown sugar 1 tsp

fresh ginger 3cm (1¼in), peeled and grated

red chilli 1, deseeded and chopped

garlic 2 cloves, peeled and crushed

freshly ground black pepper

cooked microwave jasmine rice 2 x 250g packets to serve, optional

To make the marinade, combine all the ingredients in a bowl and mix well. Add the beef, mix well, cover and marinate in the refrigerator for at least 2 hours or overnight.

Heat the oil in a flameproof casserole or saucepan over a medium heat. Add the beef in batches and fry until browned on all sides. Using a slotted spoon, remove each batch to a plate and keep it warm while you cook the remainder.

Return all the beef to the casserole, add the tomato purée and tomatoes and cook for 3–4 minutes until they start to break down. Add 1 litre (1¾ pints) of water, cover with a lid and bring to the boil. Reduce the heat and simmer for about 2 hours until the meat is tender and the sauce rich but not too thick.

Serve in small bowls, topped with shredded spring onions and mint sprigs, accompanied with jasmine rice if you like.

QR Code
Scan with a smartphone for an ingredients shopping list.

135

Beef Madras

Time required 1½ hrs plus marinating. Per portion: 547 Kcal, 33g fat (16.8g saturated)

Serves 4

To make the marinade, combine the yogurt and curry powder in a bowl. Stir in the beef, season with salt, cover and marinate in the refrigerator for 24 hours.

Heat the oil in a large lidded wok or frying pan over a medium heat. Add the bay leaf, cinnamon, cloves and cardamom pods. Stir-fry for 1 minute, then add the onion. Stir-fry for 4–5 minutes, then add the garlic, ginger, turmeric, red chilli, chilli powder and cumin. Add the marinated beef (discarding the marinade) and stir-fry for 10–15 minutes over a low heat.

Pour in the tomatoes and coconut milk, cover with a lid and bring to the boil. Then reduce the heat to low and simmer for 1 hour, stirring occasionally. Stir in the garam masala 5 minutes before the end of cooking.

Just before serving, remove the cinnamon stick, bay leaf and cardamom pods and check the seasoning, adding more salt if necessary. Drizzle with extra coconut milk and garnish with the coriander. Serve immediately with pilau rice, poppadoms and raita, if you like.

stewing beef 800g (1lb 12oz), cubed

salt

sunflower oil 2 tbsp

bay leaf 1

cinnamon stick 1

cloves 3

cardamom pods 4

onion 1 large, peeled and sliced

garlic 3 cloves, peeled and crushed

grated fresh ginger 1 tsp

ground turmeric 1 tsp

red chilli 1, split in half lengthways

hot chilli powder 2 tsp

ground cumin 2 tsp

chopped tomatoes ½ 400g can

coconut milk 300ml (½ pint), plus extra to drizzle

garam masala ¼ tsp

coriander leaves a small handful, chopped, to garnish, optional

cooked microwave pilau rice 2 x 250g packets to serve, optional

poppadoms and raita to serve, optional

for the marinade

plain yogurt 5 tbsp

Madras curry powder 3 tbsp

QR Code
Scan with a smartphone for an ingredients shopping list.

136

Boeuf Bourguignon

Time required 3 hrs. Per portion: 940 Kcal, 30g fat (9.5g saturated)

Serves 4-6

olive oil about 4 tbsp

shallots 12, peeled

rindless streaky bacon 6 rashers, cut into strips

flat mushrooms 200g (7oz), wiped and sliced

garlic 2 cloves, peeled and finely chopped

plain flour 1 tbsp

salt and freshly ground black pepper

braising steak 1kg (2lb 4oz), trimmed of excess fat and cubed

Chantenay carrots 400g (14oz), trimmed

red wine 350ml (12fl oz)

beef stock 350ml (12fl oz)

ready-made mashed potato 2–3 x 450g pots to serve, optional

QR Code
Scan with a smartphone for an ingredients shopping list.

Preheat the oven to 160°C/325°F/Gas 3. Heat 2 tablespoons of the oil in a large flameproof casserole over a medium heat. Add the shallots and cook for about 5 minutes until golden, stirring frequently. Remove from the casserole with a slotted spoon and set aside.

Add the bacon and cook for about 5 minutes until it starts to crisp, stirring occasionally. Stir in the mushrooms and garlic and cook for a further 3–5 minutes. Remove from the casserole with the slotted spoon and set aside with the shallots.

Tip the flour onto a chopping board, season with salt and pepper and mix together. Toss the cubes of beef in the seasoned flour and cook in batches, adding the remaining oil as necessary. Return the shallots, bacon, mushrooms and garlic to the casserole with the braising steak and carrots and mix well, then pour in the wine and stock. Slowly bring the mixture to the boil, stirring all the time. Cover the pan and cook in the oven for 2–2½ hours until the meat is tender.

Season with salt and pepper to taste, then serve on warmed plates with mashed potato.

139

Beef & Carrot Casserole

Time required 2½ hrs. Per portion: 551 Kcal, 28g fat (11g saturated)

Serves 4-6

Heat the oil in a large flameproof casserole or saucepan over a medium heat. Add the garlic, onion and celery and cook for 4 minutes until softened. Transfer to a plate. Put the beef in the casserole, increase the heat and fry for 5 minutes, stirring frequently, until the meat is browned all over. Return the onion mixture to the casserole. Add the stock, wine and bay leaves and season with salt and pepper. Stir to mix. Cover with a lid and bring to the boil, then reduce the heat and simmer for 1½ hours.

To make the dumplings, place the flour and baking powder in a bowl and rub in the fat until it resembles breadcrumbs. Add the cheese. Add 60-90ml (2-3fl oz) of water and use your hands to bring the mixture together and form a dough. Divide into 8 equal pieces and roll into balls.

Remove the casserole from the heat for 5 minutes, then sift in the flour and stir to thicken the gravy. Return to the heat, add the carrots and stir until the casserole comes to a simmer. Remove the bay leaves and then place the dumplings on top. Cover and cook for a further 20 minutes until the dumplings are cooked.

olive oil 1 tbsp

garlic 2 cloves, peeled and crushed

onion 1, peeled and diced

celery sticks 2, diced

chuck steak 800g (1lb 12oz), cubed

beef stock 400ml (14fl oz)

red wine 200ml (7fl oz)

bay leaves 2

salt and freshly ground black pepper

plain flour 25g (1oz)

carrots 4, peeled and cut into small chunks

for the dumplings

plain flour 200g (7oz)

baking powder 1 tsp

vegetable fat 75g (3oz)

strong Cheddar cheese 75g (3oz), grated

QR Code
Scan with a smartphone for an ingredients shopping list.

This must be comfort food at its best.
Beautifully tender beef in a rich gravy
with plump dumplings - heaven.

DESSERTS & BAKES

Figs Baked with Vanilla & Lemon

Time required 15 mins. Per portion: 169 Kcal, 5g fat (0.5g saturated)

Serves 4

figs 8 large

walnut halves 8

vanilla pod 1

caster sugar 50g (2oz)

lemon 1, grated rind only

white wine 3 tbsp

double cream or ice cream to serve, optional

QR Code
Scan with a
smartphone
for an ingredients
shopping list.

Preheat the oven to 230°C/450°F/Gas 8.

Cut a deep cross in the top of each fig so that they open up a little. Push a walnut half into each cross and then pack the figs closely together in a shallow baking dish.

Chop the vanilla pod in half and put into a food processor. Add the sugar and lemon rind and process until the pods are chopped into tiny bits. Spoon the mixture over each fig and around the dish. Moisten with white wine.

Bake in the oven for 10 minutes until the sugar melts and the figs start to caramelise. Remove from the oven and leave to cool for a few minutes before serving with cream or ice cream.

145

Spiced Berry Compote

Time required 10 mins. Per portion: 63 Kcal, 0g fat (0g saturated)

Serves 4

Put the frozen berries in a saucepan with the sugar, cinnamon and 2 tablespoons of water. Cover with a lid and simmer for 5 minutes or until the berries have defrosted and are juicy.

Blend the arrowroot or cornflour with a little cold water, then mix into the berries. Heat, stirring, until the compote has thickened. Leave to cool.

Serve the compote lightly swirled into the yogurt, with biscotti on the side, if you wish.

- **frozen summer berries** 350g (12oz)
- **caster sugar** 30g (1½oz)
- **ground cinnamon** a pinch
- **arrowroot or cornflour** 2 tsp
- **plain Greek yogurt** 600ml (1 pint), to serve
- **biscotti** to serve, optional

QR Code
Scan with a smartphone for an ingredients shopping list.

146

White Chocolate & Raspberry Fool

Time required 10 mins. Per portion: 235 Kcal, 14g fat (8.2g saturated)

Serves 2

white chocolate 40g (2½oz), broken into pieces

raspberries 125g (4½oz)

plain fromage frais 200g (7oz)

QR Code
Scan with a smartphone for an ingredients shopping list.

Melt the chocolate in a heatproof bowl set over a saucepan of gently simmering water, making sure the bottom of the bowl doesn't touch the water. Remove the bowl from the heat and leave to cool for 2 minutes.

Reserve 6 raspberries to decorate, then roughly crush the remaining raspberries with a fork.

Mix the fromage frais into the melted chocolate, then gently fold in the crushed raspberries to give a marbled effect. Spoon into 2 glasses and decorate with the reserved raspberries. Cover and chill in the refrigerator until ready to serve.

149

Meringue Nests filled with Chocolate, Cherries & Cream

Time required 20 mins plus setting time. Per portion: 244 Kcal, 16g fat (8.5g saturated)

Serves 8

Melt the chocolate in a heatpoof bowl set over a pan of gently simmering water, making sure the bottom of the bowl doesn't touch the water. Stir often. Remove the bowl from the heat and leave to cool but not set.

Put the meringues on a large plate. Then, using a teaspoon, spoon a little melted chocolate into the base of each meringue and leave to set.

Spread a sheet of greaseproof paper on a worksurface and spoon the remaining chocolate onto the paper to make 8 shards or zigzags to decorate each nest. Leave to set, chilling in the refrigerator if necessary.

Wash and dry the chocolate bowl, then pour in the cream and whisk until it is just beginning to thicken. Add the conserve and whisk again until thick. Spoon the cream into the nests and arrange the cherries on top. Gently peel the chocolate decorations from the greaseproof paper and use them to decorate the meringue nests.

dark chocolate (70% cocoa) 110g (4oz), broken into pieces

ready-made meringue nests 8

double cream 150ml (¼ pint)

berries and cherries conserve 2 tbsp

cherries 16

QR Code
Scan with a smartphone for an ingredients shopping list.

150

Simple Iced Biscuits

Time required 25 mins. Per biscuit: 85 Kcal, 5g fat (2.6g saturated)

Makes about 24 biscuits

butter 110g (4oz), cut into chunks

golden caster sugar 50g (2oz)

plain flour 125g (4½ oz)

ground almonds 50g (2oz)

almond extract a few drops

chocolate and caramel flavour icings set (a 76g set contains one milk chocolate, one white, one dark chocolate and one caramel tube of icing)

QR Code
Scan with a smartphone for an ingredients shopping list.

Preheat the oven to 180°C/350°F/Gas 4 and line two baking trays with baking parchment.

Put the butter, sugar, flour, ground almonds and almond extract into a food processor and blend until the biscuit mix starts to bind together. Turn out onto a lightly floured surface and knead gently until smooth. Roll out to the thickness of a pound coin and, using a well-floured 5.5cm (2¼in) diameter plain cutter, stamp out about 24 rounds.

Carefully transfer the biscuits to the baking trays and cook for 12–15 minutes until golden. Leave to cool on the baking sheets for a few minutes to firm up before transferring to a wire cooling rack. Once completely cold, decorate with zigzags, swirls, names or dots using the different flavoured icings.

153

Cinnamon & Raisin Flapjacks

Time required 40 mins. Per portion: 200 Kcal, 9g fat (5.1g saturated)

Makes 16 squares

Preheat the oven to 160°C/325°F/Gas 3 and grease and line a 20cm (8in) square tin.

Put the butter, sugar, syrup and cinnamon into a large heavy-based saucepan and melt over a medium-low heat, stirring occasionally. Remove from the heat and mix in the oats and raisins.

Tip the mixture into the prepared tin and spread evenly. Lightly press the mixture down with the back of the spoon to level the surface, then bake for 25–30 minutes until the flapjacks are turning golden brown around the edges.

Remove from the oven and leave to cool for 10 minutes. Carefully mark the mixture into 16 squares with a knife. Leave until cold before removing from the tin and cutting fully into squares or bars. Store in an airtight container.

butter 150g (5oz)

soft light brown sugar 110g (4oz)

golden syrup 110g (4oz)

ground cinnamon ¼-½ tsp

porridge oats 275g (10oz)

raisins 110g (4oz)

QR Code
Scan with a smartphone for an ingredients shopping list.

Apricot & Almond Bake

Time required 40 mins. Per portion: 450 Kcal, 23g fat (6.8g saturated)

Serves 4-6

apricot halves 2 x 410g cans, drained

for the almond batter

plain flour 200g (7oz)

baking powder 1 tbsp

salt a pinch

golden caster sugar 50g (2oz)

ground almonds 110g (4oz)

milk about 350ml (12fl oz)

unsalted butter 50g (2oz), melted

whole blanched almonds 30g (1½oz)

vanilla ice cream to serve, optional

QR Code
Scan with a
smartphone
for an ingredients
shopping list.

Preheat the oven to 190°C/375°F/Gas 5 and grease a large baking tin.

To make the batter, sift together the flour, baking powder and salt into a bowl and mix with the sugar. Stir in the ground almonds, milk and melted butter and whisk until the mixture is smooth and thick. Pour the batter into the prepared baking tin, then push in the apricots, cut-side up, in a higgledy-piggledy manner and slightly at an angle all over. Place a whole almond inside each apricot.

Bake for 25–30 minutes in the middle of the oven until it is risen and golden. Remove from the oven and allow to cool slightly before serving with ice cream.

Baked Apples & Pears

Time required 40 mins. Per portion: 545 Kcal, 32g fat (16.5g saturated)

Serves 2

Preheat the oven to 200°C/400°F/Gas 6.

Peel the apples. If necessary, trim the bottom slightly so they sit flat. Remove the cores with a small knife or a corer. Using a small spoon, scrape out some apple to make space for more stuffing. Don't go all the way down to the bottom. Peel the pear, then halve and scoop out the core.

Put the hazelnuts, prunes and figs in a small bowl and stir well. Then arrange the apples and pear halves in a baking dish and stuff the fruit mixture into the cavities, mounding it at the top. Top each with a light sprinkling of cinnamon and a knob of butter then trickle over a teaspoon of honey. Cover with foil.

Bake in the oven for 20 minutes, then remove the foil and continue baking for a further 10–15 minutes until the fruit is just golden. Divide the apples and pears carefully between the plates and pour over any pan juices. Serve warm, with Greek yogurt.

apples 2, preferably Cox or Braeburn

just-ripe pear 1, preferably Conference

whole hazelnuts 20g (¾oz), coarsely chopped

soft prunes 6, chopped

dried figs 4–5, chopped

ground cinnamon a pinch

unsalted butter 50g (2oz)

runny honey 4 tsp

plain Greek yogurt to serve, optional

QR Code
Scan with a smartphone for an ingredients shopping list.

158

*This American classic makes perfect
comfort food. You can change the fruit
according to the season.*

Peach Cobbler

Time required 45 mins. Per portion: 450 Kcal, 25g fat (14.8g saturated)

Serves 6

just-ripe peaches 6

plain flour 1 tbsp

lemon juice 1 tbsp

runny honey 3 tbsp

cream or vanilla ice cream to serve, optional

for the cobbler topping

plain flour 175g (6oz)

caster sugar 50g (2oz), plus 2–3 tbsp for sprinkling

baking powder 1 tsp

bicarbonate of soda ¼ tsp

salt a pinch

unsalted butter 50g (2oz)

double cream 125ml (4fl oz)

crème fraîche 5 tbsp

QR Code
Scan with a smartphone for an ingredients shopping list.

Preheat the oven to 190°C/375°F/Gas 5.

Cut the peaches in half, remove the stones, and then cut each half into three slices. Put them in a shallow baking dish, sprinkle with the flour and toss well to coat evenly. Add the lemon juice and honey and stir. Set aside.

Put the flour, sugar, baking powder, bicarbonate of soda and salt in a large bowl and mix well. Add the butter and mix with your fingertips until the mixture resembles coarse crumbs. Using a fork, stir in the cream and crème fraîche until blended – use your hands at the end if necessary – the mixture should be sticky, thick and not that easy to blend.

Drop spoonfuls of the mixture on top of the peaches, leaving gaps to expose the fruit. Sprinkle 2–3 tablespoons of sugar on top, then bake in the oven for 25–35 minutes until golden (cover with foil if the topping is browning too much before the peaches are cooked). Serve warm with cream or ice cream.

161

Simple Plum Crumble

Time required 50 mins. Per portion: 291 Kcal, 11g fat (6.6g saturated)

Serves 4-6

Preheat the oven to 180°C/350°F/Gas 4 and set a baking tray on the middle shelf to heat.

Cut the plums in half and remove the stones, then cut the halves into quarters if they are very large. Toss them with the sugar and tip them into an ovenproof baking dish.

To make the crumble topping, rub the butter into the flour with the salt until it resembles rough breadcrumbs. Stir in the sugar.

Lightly scatter the topping mixture over the plums. Place the dish on the baking tray in the oven and bake for 40–45 minutes until golden brown. Remove from the oven and serve warm with cream.

plums 8–10
caster sugar 4–5 tbsp

for the crumble topping
unsalted butter 75g (3oz), chilled
plain flour 175g (6oz)
salt a pinch
caster sugar 50g (2oz)
single cream to serve, optional

QR Code
Scan with a smartphone for an ingredients shopping list.

Ginger & Marmalade Steamed Pudding

Time required 1¾ hrs. Per portion: 323 Kcal, 18g fat (10.5g saturated)

Serves 6-8

thin-cut marmalade 2 tbsp

butter 150g (5oz), softened

caster sugar 150g (5oz)

eggs 3, lightly beaten

plain flour 150g (5oz)

baking powder 1 tsp

ground ginger 1½ tsp

custard to serve, optional

QR Code
Scan with a smartphone for an ingredients shopping list.

Grease a 1 litre (1¾ pint) pudding basin and line the base with greaseproof paper. Put a large piece of foil on top of a piece of greaseproof paper of the same size and fold along the centre to make a pleat, which will allow for steam.

Spread 1 tablespoon of the marmalade evenly over the base of the pudding basin. In a large bowl, thoroughly beat together all the remaining ingredients with a hand-held electric whisk. Spoon the pudding batter into the prepared basin and level the surface. Cover the top of the basin with the greaseproof paper and foil and securely tie under the lip of the basin with string.

Place the bowl on a heatproof saucer in the base of a large deep saucepan. Lower in the pudding and pour in enough water to come halfway up the sides of the basin. Cover the saucepan and bring to the boil, then reduce the heat and simmer for 1½ hours, topping up the water if necessary.

Lift the pudding out, using the string, and leave it to stand for 5 minutes. Then turn the pudding out onto a warmed plate, top with another tablespoon of marmalade and serve warm with custard.

Lemon Tart

Time required 1½ hrs. Per portion: 473 Kcal, 29g fat (11.7g saturated)

Serves 8

Preheat the oven to 190°C/375°F/Gas 5 and pop a baking sheet in the oven to heat up.

Roll out the pastry on a lightly floured surface to a few centimetres larger than the base and sides of a 23cm (9in) diameter fluted loose-bottomed flan tin. Line the tin with the pastry, pressing it into the corners of the flutes. Don't trim the rim of the pastry. Prick the base and chill for 10 minutes.

Line the pastry case with foil or baking parchment and fill with baking beans. Then put the flan tin on the hot baking sheet and bake blind for 10 minutes. Remove the flan from the oven, take out the beans and paper and, using a rolling pin or sharp knife, roll over the top of the tin to remove any extra pastry. Bake for a further 10 minutes or until the pastry is crisp. Remove from the oven. Reduce the oven temperature to 140°C/275°F/Gas 1.

To make the filling, whisk the eggs with the sugar and lemon zest in a large jug. Whisk in the lemon juice followed by the cream.

Pop the cooked pastry case back on the baking sheet and pour the filling into the case. Bake for 30–40 minutes until the mixture is just set. There should still be a slight wobble in the centre. Remove the tart from the oven and leave it to cool, then remove from the tin and set on a plate. Serve cold dusted with icing sugar and a few raspberries for decoration, if using.

ready-made sweet dessert pastry 375g packet

eggs 5 large

caster sugar 200g (7oz)

lemons 3, grated rind only

fresh lemon juice 150ml (¼ pint)

double cream 150ml (¼ pint)

icing sugar for dusting, optional

raspberries to decorate, optional

QR Code
Scan with a smartphone for an ingredients shopping list.

Mini Carrot Cakes

Time required 45 mins plus cooling. Per portion: 466 Kcal, 22g fat (6.5g saturated)

Makes 12 cakes

bananas 2

carrots 175g (6oz), peeled and finely grated

self-raising flour 275g (10oz)

baking powder 1 tsp

ground mixed spice 1 tsp

soft light brown sugar 175g (6oz)

eggs 3, beaten

sunflower oil 175ml (6fl oz)

for the topping

butter 50g (2oz), softened

icing sugar 300g (11oz), sifted

full fat soft cheese 125g (4½oz)

ready-made chocolate carrot decorations 1 packet with 12 carrots

QR Code
Scan with a smartphone for an ingredients shopping list.

Preheat the oven to 180°C/350°F/Gas 4 and thoroughly oil a 12-hole non-stick muffin tin.

Mash the bananas in a large bowl, then stir in the carrots followed by the remaining ingredients. Beat well with a wooden spoon.

Pour the mixture into the muffin tins, filling each hole to the top. Bake for 20–30 minutes until golden and well risen, then remove from the oven and leave to cool in the tin for 5 minutes before turning out onto a wire rack to cool completely.

For the icing, using a wooden spoon beat together the butter and sugar until the consistency of coarse breadcrumbs. Then beat in the soft cheese and continue beating until the icing is soft and fluffy. Generously swirl the icing on top of each cake and decorate with a ready-made carrot.

169

Parkin

Time required 1¼ hrs. Per portion: 433 Kcal, 17g fat (9.6g saturated)

Makes 1 cake; 9 squares

Preheat the oven to 170°C/325°F/Gas 3. Grease and line an 18cm (7in) square deep cake tin.

Put the syrup, butter and sugar in a microwave-proof bowl and microwave on high for 1½–2 minutes, stirring after 1 minute, until the mixture has just melted. Leave it to cool a little.

Add the remaining ingredients to the syrupy butter and beat well until thoroughly mixed. Pour into the prepared tin and bake for 50–55 minutes until firm to touch. Cool in the tin for 15 minutes, then turn out onto a wire rack. Wrap in cling film and eat within 2 days of baking.

- **golden syrup** 175g (6oz)
- **butter** 150g (5oz)
- **soft light brown sugar** 110g (4oz)
- **self-raising flour** 175g (6oz)
- **ground ginger** 1 tsp
- **ground mixed spice** 1 tsp
- **crystallised stem ginger** 2 tbsp, chopped
- **medium oatmeal** 250g (9oz)
- **egg** 1
- **milk** 150ml (¼ pint)
- **bicarbonate of soda** 1 tsp

QR Code
Scan with a smartphone for an ingredients shopping list.

170

Executive Editor	Nick Rowe
Managing Editor	Emily Davenport
Editor	Emma Callery
Designer	Graham Meigh
Photographers	Steve Lee (18-21, 25, 30, 33-8, 54, 58-62, 78, 83, 102-6, 113, 114, 118, 125, 126, 133, 138, 144, 151-5, 164-171)
	Loupe Images/Caroline Arber (129, 141)
	Loupe Images/Martin Brigdale (89, 97, 121)
	Loupe Images/Peter Cassidy (26, 53, 70, 90, 158, 163)
	Loupe Images/Nicki Dowey (98)
	Loupe Images/Tara Fisher (45)
	Loupe Images/Richard Jung (front cover, 46, 65, 66, 69, 74, 85, 86, 101)
	Loupe Images/David Munns (22, 42, 81, 109, 122, 159, 160)
	Loupe Images/Noel Murphy (77, 82)
	Loupe Images/William Reavell (29, 49, 57, 73, 94, 110, 117, 134, 147, 148)
	Loupe Images/Debi Treloar (130)
	Loupe Images/Kate Whitaker (50, 137)
Food Stylist	Sara Lewis
Props Stylist	Jo Harris

Recipes created by

Lucy Knox (18-21, 32-39, 55, 59-63, 79, 92, 103, 105, 112, 115, 124, 127, 132, 139, 150-4, 165-170)	
Nadia Arumugam (47, 64, 67, 68, 75)	Rachael Anne Hill (28, 48, 72, 99, 146, 149)
Pat Alburey (31)	Elsa Petersen-Schepelern (27, 131)
Ghillie Başan (96)	Louise Pickford (52, 71)
Tamsin Burnett-Hall (28, 48, 72, 146, 149)	Jennie Shapter (44)
Maxine Clark (76, 83, 88, 91, 145, 157, 162)	Sonia Stevenson (56, 111, 135)
Ross Dobson (84, 87, 100)	Sunil Vijayakar (51, 136)
Silvana Franco (107)	Fran Warde (119, 128, 140)
Tonia George (95, 116)	Laura Washburn (23, 43, 80, 108, 120, 123, 158, 161)
Katherine Hawkins (24)	

Proof Reader	Aune Butt	
Indexer	Christine Bernstein	
Nutritional consultant	Dr Wendy Doyle	
Recipe testers	Richard Davenport	Chris Perry
	Barbara Glimmerveen	Laura Pickering
	Katy Hackforth	Kirstin Shankland
	Lucy Padget	Gudrun Waskett
Production	Cath Linter	

Eaglemoss Consumer Publications Ltd
Electra House, Electra Way, Crewe, Cheshire, CW1 6WZ
Telephone 01270 270050
Website www.dairydiary.co.uk

First printed May 2013
© Eaglemoss Consumer Publications Ltd
ISBN-13: 978-0-9571772-0-8

123456789

Whilst every care has been taken in compiling the information in this book, the publishers cannot accept responsibility for any errors, in advertent or not, that may be found or may occur at some time in the future owing to changes in legislation or for any other reason.